Web Indicators for Research Evaluation

A Practical Guide

Synthesis Lectures on Information Concepts, Retrieval, and Services

Gary Marchionini, *University of North Carolina, Chapel Hill*

Synthesis Lectures on Information Concepts, Retrieval, and Services publishes short books on topics pertaining to information science and applications of technology to information discovery, production, distribution, and management. Potential topics include: data models, indexing theory and algorithms, classification, information architecture, information economics, privacy and identity, scholarly communication, bibliometrics and webometrics, personal information management, human information behavior, digital libraries, archives and preservation, cultural informatics, information retrieval evaluation, data fusion, relevance feedback, recommendation systems, question answering, natural language processing for retrieval, text summarization, multimedia retrieval, multilingual retrieval, and exploratory search.

Synthesis Lectures on Information Concepts, Retrieval, and Services

Gary Marchionini, *University of North Carolina, Chapel Hill*

Synthesis Lectures on Information Concepts, Retrieval, and Services publishes short books on topics pertaining to information science and applications of technology to information discovery, production, distribution, and management. Potential topics include: data models, indexing theory and algorithms, classification, information architecture, information economics, privacy and identity, scholarly communication, bibliometrics and webometrics, personal information management, human information behavior, digital libraries, archives and preservation, cultural informatics, information retrieval evaluation, data fusion, relevance feedback, recommendation systems, question answering, natural language processing for retrieval, text summarization, multimedia retrieval, multilingual retrieval, and exploratory search.

Automated Metadata in Multimedia Information Systems: Creation, Refinement, Use in Surrogates, and Evaluation
Michael G. Christel

Web Indicators for Research Evaluation: A Practical
Guide Michael Thelwall

ISBN: 978-3-031-01176-4   print
ISBN: 978-3-031-02304-0   ebook

DOI 10.1007/978-3-031-02304-0

A Publication in the Springer series
SYNTHESIS LECTURES ON INFORMATION CONCEPTS, RETRIEVAL, AND SERVICES #52

Series Editor: Gary Marchionini, University of North Carolina, Chapel Hill

Series ISSN 1947-945X Print   1947-9468 Electronic

Web Indicators for Research Evaluation

A Practical Guide

Michael Thelwall
University of Wolverhampton

SYNTHESIS LECTURES ON INFORMATION CONCEPTS, RETRIEVAL, AND SERVICES #52

ABSTRACT

In recent years there has been an increasing demand for research evaluation within universities and other research-based organisations. In parallel, there has been an increasing recognition that traditional citation-based indicators are not able to reflect the societal impacts of research and are slow to appear. This has led to the creation of new indicators for different types of research impact as well as timelier indicators, mainly derived from the Web. These indicators have been called altmetrics, webometrics or just web metrics. This book describes and evaluates a range of web indicators for aspects of societal or scholarly impact, discusses the theory and practice of using and evaluating web indicators for research assessment and outlines practical strategies for obtaining many web indicators. In addition to describing impact indicators for traditional scholarly outputs, such as journal articles and monographs, it also covers indicators for videos, datasets, software and other non-standard scholarly outputs. The book describes strategies to analyse web indicators for individual publications as well as to compare the impacts of groups of publications. The practical part of the book includes descriptions of how to use the free software Webometric Analyst to gather and analyse web data. This book is written for information science undergraduate and Master's students that are learning about alternative indicators or scientometrics as well as Ph.D. students and other researchers and practitioners using indicators to help assess research impact or to study scholarly communication.

KEYWORDS

web indicators, altmetrics, webometrics, alternative indicators, scientometrics, bibliometrics, scholarly communication, social media metrics

Contents

CHAPTER   1

Introduction

The need for research evaluation has increased dramatically in recent decades. A major source of demand is from organisations involved in the research process that need to assess the value of academic research (e.g., Wilsdon, 2016; www.snowballmetrics.com). These include:

- governments judging the effect of recent policy changes;

- governments and funding bodies interested in the value for money of their research spending;

- higher education funders dividing annual block grants between universities, such as through the UK Research Excellence Framework (REF);

- universities deciding how to share out budgets between departments;

- funding councils allocating project grants;

- departments choosing researchers to appoint and promote;

- libraries renewing journal subscriptions; and

- university managers, administrators, publishers or other stakeholders seeking to second guess or plan for the outcomes of any of the above.

This final reason is particularly important because any evaluation that has substantial financial implications triggers a need to plan in the affected organisations. This gives them a degree of control over, or early warning about, the outcomes. For example, probably all UK universities conducted mock REF exercises in the years before submitting to REF2014 (e.g., Gray, 2015; Owens, 2013) and had a dedicated team of REF administrators and academics in order to maximise their university's scores. Individual researchers also sometimes need to evaluate research to plan for future organisational assessments or for a variety of different purposes.

- To self-assess their progress

- To choose a venue in which to publish their work

- To select articles to read from a large collection that match their digital library search

- To select articles to read from a new issue of a journal or from recent additions to a digital repository

Scholars who investigate science itself may also need to assess bodies of scholarship. Even though many scholars produce intangible knowledge and understanding, most evaluations take the initial simplifying step of focusing exclusively or primarily on tangible outputs, such as articles, chapters and books.

Assessments that focus on academic outputs can be slow and complex. This is because scholars tend to produce work that is densely written, understandable to a small number of people, and can only be fully evaluated within the context of a large pool of similar outputs (e.g., for their level of novelty and relative strength of methods). Even experts with the background knowledge to understand individual publications need time to read them and may disagree on their merits. For these reasons it is difficult for non-experts to properly assess the work of scholars, for peers to evaluate the multiple outputs of large groups of researchers and for interested parties to sift through masses of published work in order to find the most important and relevant items. Thus, there is a seemingly impossible need to evaluate academic research *without reading it*.

Many in the past have resorted to citation counts to help with this task with the hypothesis that more cited works tend to be better. From this assumption, it follows that citation counts can be used as a convenient proxy for academic impact or quality. This belief is supported by the argument that scientists cite to acknowledge influential prior work so that highly cited papers are important for the progress of science (Merton, 1973). While this is broadly true in many areas of scholarship, each document's references are likely to be an incomplete and biased reflection of the influences on the research (MacRoberts and MacRoberts, 1989). Thus, citation counts can be misleading in individual cases even though in aggregate they may be reasonable indicators of academic impact in many fields (van Raan, 1998; Moed, 2005). Moreover, there is a substantial time lag between a scholar conducting research and their outputs having enough citations to estimate their citation impact.

A more fundamental weakness of citation counts is that governments and other funders rarely want to finance research for its own sake. Instead, scholarship is a means to an end, such as more effective higher education, enhanced international competitiveness, improved public health and national cultural enrichment. In this context, citation counts appear to be measuring the wrong research outcome. They have been adopted in the past due to a lack of alternatives and arguments by academics that research excellence would itself naturally lead to the desired societal benefits. Nevertheless, there is ongoing pressure for indicators that will more directly reflect valuable research application types.

In parallel with the need to evaluate the non-academic impacts of research is the need to evaluate non-standard research outputs. Academia is increasingly complex and digitised (Meyer and Schroeder, 2015), with individual scholars and groups producing outputs of types that are often ignored in research assessments. For example, while evaluations may focus on academic journal articles and books, scholars may also produce software, databases, videos, blogs and other artefacts.

These can be central to a research field, as in the case of biodiversity and chemical databases, machine learning software environments and natural language processing toolkits. They can also make helpful contributions to education, as in the case of videos exploring the normally unseen work of scientists (www.test-tube.org.uk). Non-standard outputs can also support science as a whole as in the case of the blog posts and newspaper articles of Professor Stephen Curry (www.theguardian.com/profile/stephen-curry), which promote and explain issues of general importance to researchers. There is little hope that citation counts can be useful in evaluating many of these contributions, although there are drives to encourage researchers to formally cite the software and data that they use in their studies.

A similar issue is that academics are increasingly called upon to directly engage with potential end users of their research and to seek ways in which their expertise can help society. As an example, the Flanders Marine Institute assesses local marine biodiversity, has a school outreach programme and produces publications aimed at the local fishing industry, including *Compendium Coast and Sea*, which aims to "aggregate objective and scientifically-underpinned information and data from Flemish/Belgian marine and maritime research" (www.vliz.be/en/compendium-coast-and-sea). Similarly, the Oxford Internet Institute produces a periodic survey of internet use in the UK as a service for the community (oxis.oii.ox.ac.uk) and the *Stern Review on the Economics of Climate Change* is a high-profile example of a huge amount of academic work used to directly inform government policy. Any indicators that could help to assess the impact of such activities would be valuable for the funders that need to check that they are getting value for money.

A potential solution to the above problems has appeared in the form of the web. The rise of the web to become embedded in the work of scholars and wider society has created a situation in which there is easily accessible public online evidence of research impacts that could be exploited for new indicators. While none of the new indicators can deal with all research evaluation needs, some can reflect important non-academic types of impact or can be applied to non-standard outputs. Questions such as the following have triggered a particular interest in web indicators.

- Do tweet counts reflect the degree of public interest in research?

- Do citations from online patents reflect commercial technology transfer?

- Can mentions in the online grey literature provide evidence of policy impacts?

- Could the fast publishing nature of the web make it possible to generate early impact indicators?

There are strong opponents of the use of impact indicators and particular types of web indicators (Colquhoun and Plested, 2014) and some have argued that their value has been exaggerated (Barnes, 2015). Thus, it is important to critically evaluate the value of web indicators, to develop effective methods to use them and theory to help interpret them.

This book describes and evaluates a range of web indicators, drawing upon relevant empirical studies. It takes a critical perspective, emphasising the generic and specific limitations of each indicator so that they can be used with appropriate care. It also takes a positive approach by describing contexts in which web indicators can be useful and providing practical help with calculating them.

1.1   INDICATOR TERMINOLOGY AND INTERPRETATION

Indicator terminology is used somewhat interchangeably in practice, but it is useful to give precise definitions for this book. Here, an **indicator** is a number that is used or developed to point to the direction or level of achievement of an entity of any sort. It may be a simple individual number, such as a tweet count, or the result of a mathematical formula applied to a set of numbers, such as the arithmetic mean or geometric mean. This definition excludes non-numerical entities, such as pictures and network diagrams, although indicators can be represented by graphs or within network diagrams. In society, a well-known indicator is the gross domestic product, which provides evidence of national economic strength. In the UK, the retail price index (RPI) calculated by the Office for National Statistics (ONS) estimates the change in purchasing power of money for consumers by monitoring the average price of a sample of retail goods and services. Its inflation values are widely used despite being misleading for consumers who purchase goods or services that are not on the list and that have a different pattern of price changes, such as luxury or black market goods. It can also be misleading overall if an essential good or service that is not on the list exhibits a large price change that is out of line with other goods and services due to a market collapse or flooding. Despite the demonstrable failings of the RPI it is still a useful indicator of the purchasing power of money for typical consumers. This leads to the following conclusion.

> An indicator does not have to be very accurate to be useful as long as, on average, higher values associate with higher levels of the quantity being assessed.

This point is important because a common criticism of citation counts (and, by extension, most web indicators) is that research can be cited for negative reasons, such as to criticise methods or findings (MacRoberts and MacRoberts, 1996). Despite this, if indicators tend to give scores that agree to a large extent with human judgements then it would be reasonable to replace human judgements with them when a decision is not important enough to justify the time necessary for experts to read the articles in question.

> Indicators can be useful when the value of an assessment is not great enough to justify the time needed by experts to make human judgements.

For decisions that are important enough to require expert judgements on a collection of outputs, indicators can still be useful to cross-check the expert opinions in order to either highlight areas in which they may have overlooked excellence or overrated poor research—although the experts should make the final decision. Indicators may also be used to help look for evidence of systematic biases in human judgements, such as on the basis of author gender, disability or ethnicity. For example, if the outputs of female academics tended to have indicator scores that were double those of male academics before being judged excellent then this should trigger gender bias investigations.

Indicators can be useful to support or cross-check expert human judgements.

Indicators can support specific impact claims by academics for individual outputs. For example, someone might argue that devoting all of their research time to a blog is valuable because of the large audience that it attracts. They could use blog access statistics to support this claim.

Indicators can support the impact claims of practicing researchers.

Indicators can also be preferable to human judgements for theoretical analyses of science itself and of systemic biases, such as in terms of the career success of researchers by gender, disability or ethnicity.

Indicators can be preferable to expert human judgements for system-level analyses.

Although perfect accuracy is not essential for any of these tasks, increased accuracy is clearly desirable for any indicator and increases the range of tasks for which it is useful.

1.2   METRICS AND INDICATORS

It is useful to distinguish between the terms *metric* and *indicator*, even though the difference between them is one of perspective and there are different uses of both terms in society and academia (e.g., Lazarsfeld, 1958; Hubbard, 2014). Both *metric* and *measure* can cause confusion in a scientometric context because a commonsense interpretation is that if something has been *measured* then the measurement will be essentially exact (e.g., Hubbard, 2014, p. 30). In science (including the social sciences), however, a measurement usually has a more technical interpretation as a quantitative entity that reduces uncertainty to any degree at all, and can incorporate even large errors (Hubbard, 2014, p. 32). Thus, for example, if it is possible to show that knowing the number of web citations received by an article reduces the degree of uncertainty about whether it is a good quality article or not then it would be scientifically reasonable to describe web citation counts as a *measure* of (research) quality. Nevertheless, it would be unreasonable from a commonsense perspective to describe web citation counts as a measure of quality because highly cited articles can be poor and so the web citation count measurement can have very large errors. The same logic also holds for traditional citation counts and all web indicators. Thus, the terms *measurement* and *metric* carry commonsense connotations of accuracy, even though this is not a scientific property of their common definitions.

For research evaluation purposes, although not common practice, it would be helpful to reserve the terms *metric* and *measurement* for things that have a reasonable degree of accuracy. This would reduce the frequent commonsense objections to indicators on the basis of their large obvious errors. These objections often take the form of individual cases of large discrepancies, such as highly cited false papers, or evidence of bias. For example, the retweet count reported by Twitter is a retweet metric for the number of times that a tweet has been retweeted. Presumably this number tends to be reasonably accurate even though it may occasionally be wrong if very recent retweets are ignored by the software that calculates it. In contrast, it could be misleading (although not technically incorrect) to describe the retweet count as a popularity *metric* in Twitter because a tweet may be highly retweeted by spammers and so retweet counts can give highly inaccurate popularity estimates in some cases.

It is also helpful in research evaluations to avoid using terminology with connotations of accuracy because the outcomes may be used by non-experts to judge researchers and these non-experts may apply a commonsense interpretation. This may lead to unwarranted accuracy assumptions (e.g., that all articles in journals with high impact factors are excellent) or the rejection of all data because of occasional obvious large errors. Both of these over-interpretations are reasonable from a commonsense understanding of the term *measure*.

In contrast, the term *indicator* does not carry the strong commonsense connotations of precision that the terms measure and metric do. Although (again) not common practice, it is helpful in research evaluation to use *indicator* for any quantitative entity that is known or believed to associate with the phenomenon of interest even if it does not accurately measure it. In the above case retweet counts could be described as a popularity *indicator* within Twitter because it seems reasonable to believe that, in general, more popular tweets will be retweeted more than less popular tweets. Confusingly, an indicator can be a (commonsense) metric for one thing but not another. The counts of tweets citing an article is a metric of how often the article is tweeted, and may be an indicator of the impact of the article but should not be described as an impact metric for articles because counting tweets does not accurately measure the impact of an article. In this book, the term *metric* will be used for indicators when discussing that they measure something (other than research impact) with a reasonable degree of accuracy.

> For research evaluation it is better to use the term *indicator* than the terms *metric* or *measurement* for quantities that can have large errors. This will help to reduce confusion from non-experts who may assume that metrics and measurements should be accurate.

The definition of an indicator does not include any cause-and-effect requirement with the type of impact assessed. While showing that such a relationship is present would help to interpret the meaning of a web indicator, it is not necessary. If there is an unknown, weak or no cause-and-effect relationship then extra caution should be used when interpreting indicator values, however.

In practice, this means that an indicator should not be used as the primary source of evidence, if possible, and that its values should be checked for anomalies in each application.

Additional problems arise when indicators are used to help assess researchers, who may focus on the indicator rather than the goal of the assessment. In a policy context, whenever an indicator is publicly selected in advance of an evaluation then getting higher indicator values is desirable for those evaluated or other stakeholders. If there is not a straightforward and robust cause-and-effect relationship then there will be a behaviour change in the direction of the indicator rather than in the direction of the factor that it is an indicator of (e.g., getting friends to retweet rather than trying to write more popular outputs). Thus, consideration of the consequences of using indicators is needed as well as information about their properties.

> The consequence of the use of an indicator on the behaviour of those assessed must be thought through before the indicator is used.

A partial exception to the above is for "surprise" evaluations in which the indicators to be used are not known in advance but are requested by the judges performing the assessment. In such cases, it is too late for those assessed to modify their behaviour but there may still be behaviour change after the assessment if they anticipate the use of similar indicators in a future assessment.

1.3   WEB INDICATORS

This book focuses on academic and academic-related indicators derived from the web. Citation counts from the Web of Science and Scopus are the most researched type of academic indicator and are the benchmark for discussing alternative indicators. Here, a **web indicator** is a number that is (a) intended to associate with an aspect of research performance or impact, and that is (b) derived from the web and not in any way from counts of citations from academic journal articles. This excludes citation counts from the Web of Science and Scopus (even though they are on the web) as well as formulae that process citation counts, such as the Journal Impact Factor (Garfield, 1999) and field-normalised citation counts (Waltman et al., 2011). In practice, within this book, web indicators always relate to tangible academic-related outputs, such as journal articles, scholar-produced videos, or monographs. They can reflect general, academic, educational, commercial, organisational or information impact.

There are many different types of web indicators. The most well-known type, called social media metrics or altmetrics (Priem et al., 2011; see also: Holmberg, 2015), are derived from social websites, such as Twitter, that are free to join and open to the public. Social media metrics are typically collected by a computer program through an applications programming interface (API), and this facility has made them relatively easy to collect. A more general term is *webometrics* (Almind and Ingwersen, 1997), which originally referred to all indicators derived from the public web and now also describes a research field of the same name. The word *webometrics* is currently used for indicators derived from the web except for social media metrics. Usage metrics, in contrast, give evidence of how often a document or other resource has been viewed, downloaded or otherwise accessed online (Kurtz and Bollen, 2010). Usage metrics may be derived from the web or social web, overlapping with the previous two classes, or may be derived from web server log files, which are about the web but are not themselves part of the public web or social web. These are included in this book for completeness.

This book does not cover alternative indicators that are derived primarily from non-web sources, such as in the case of some patent and reputation indicators.

1.4   BOOK-SPECIFIC INDICATORS

Although most research into web indicators has focused on journal articles, in the arts, humanities and some social sciences, important scholarly output types include monographs, edited books and book chapters. While it is possible to count citations to books from journal articles in traditional citation indexes, such citations do not reflect the scholarly and other impacts of books well (Cronin et al., 1997). This is because books can target book-based research fields. The situation has been partly remedied by the Web of Science and Scopus indexing substantial numbers of books, but both cover only a small, English-focused subset of the world's academic output and there are better web indicator solutions.

Books in general can productively be used in many ways that do not lead to new journal citations, such as supporting education, informing policy, professional practice and health behaviours, and culturally enriching the reader. Books may also further lines of research that are predominantly published in monographs and book chapters. In addition, citation practices are different in the humanities, with serendipitous citations being common (Stone, 1982) even though they do not reflect the academic contributions of the cited works. Nevertheless, it seems reasonable to believe that important books would tend to be highly cited, whether by other books or by journal articles. The best source of data about citations to books is therefore a huge book database, and Google Books is the logical choice for this. Web indicators can be particularly helpful for books because of the multidimensional ways in which they can have impacts (Halevi et al., 2016).

It is particularly useful to have evidence of the number of readers for a book since books do not need to generate citations in order to have an impact, but they must at least be read first. The ideal book readership evidence would be book sales (print and electronic) added to library loans but sales information does not seem to be released by publishers and may not be reliable between publishers. Similarly, library loan information does not seem to be ever put in the public domain. Proxy readership indicators are therefore needed. Mendeley reader counts would be a logical choice but users seem to rarely register books on the site. One public source of sales-related data, albeit only from specific online bookstores, is the sales rank published by sites like Amazon.com. For libraries, although lending information is not shared, except perhaps with the security agencies, catalog information is usually public and so it is possible to count the library holdings of a book as a proxy indicator of the likely extent of its readership.

1.5   INDICATORS FOR NON-STANDARD SCHOLARLY OUTPUTS

Data, software, videos, blogs, reports and images are important outputs of some scholars' research, and web indicators, such as view or download counts, are a natural source of impact evidence for them. Non-standard scholarly outputs that give value to the scholarly community need to be recognised so that researchers continue to create them and do not divert their attentions to less valuable but more recognised activities. This book briefly discusses indicators for a range of different types of academic output. The brief coverage is partly due to the scarcity of relevant investigations and partly because, as discussed in the conclusions, web indicators for non-standard outputs are best used in a simple way.

The magnitude of any indicator should be interpreted relative to the context in which it is expected to be used and this can vary enormously for non-standard scholarly outputs. In theory, the impact of a resource should be the number of uses times the average value of each use. On this basis, for example, an icon library with millions of fairly trivial uses could be fairly compared against a video illustrating a new separation technique for conjoined twins that may only have a few viewers but each one might save two lives. Such calculations are impossible because the users of a resource are often unknown and the value of their uses would typically be impossible or impractical to calculate. Of course, the same is true for citations: while some are fairly trivial, others can be vital to new studies. Nevertheless, the magnitude of the difference is much larger for most resource types, except perhaps datasets because it is difficult to imagine that there are many trivial uses of datasets. Because of this, it seems most useful to employ web indicators to individual resources or homogenous collections of resources (e.g., Haran and Poliakoff, 2011) accompanied by a textual explanation of the context. The case for the value of an indicator could be strengthened if it could be benchmarked against equivalent values for resources of a similar type and intended audience. This would allow resource owners to make claims such as "X is the most downloaded free software for counting angels on pinheads" or "Our video of fly eggs hatching in horse manure has been viewed twice as often as video of the same event that is also aimed at school pupils." Unfortunately, benchmarking is difficult in practice because the well-known resources tend to be the successful minority while the failures are unknown and difficult to find.

1.6   DISCIPLINARY AND TIME DIFFERENCES

The typical values of all indicator data vary by field and year (see Section 9.3). Because of this, indicators should not be calculated for sets of articles from multiple fields and years and should not be compared between fields and years. More sophisticated indicators are needed to compare between fields and years and these are discussed in Chapter 9.

> Most indicators should not be compared between fields because of disciplinary differences. Most indicators should not be compared between years because of time differences.

1.7   OVERVIEW AND INTENDED AUDIENCE

This book describes a range of web indicators for different impact types, covers the theory and practice of using web indicators for research assessment and outlines practical strategies for obtaining many web indicators. It discusses the use of indicators to help evaluate traditional scholarly outputs, such as journal articles and monographs, as well as for other types of online scholarly outputs, such as videos, datasets and software. The book also describes how to evaluate collections of such outputs, such as those produced by individuals, groups and institutions.

This book is aimed at undergraduate and Master's degree students within information science who are learning about alternative indicators or scientometrics, as well as Ph.D. students, researchers and practitioners who are using, or would like to use, alternative indicators for academic impact evaluations or to study scholarly communication. The first part is also aimed at policy makers and research administrators who need to know which indicators to use and how to interpret their values. In contrast to a volume on webometric methods for investigating sets of websites (Thelwall, 2009), and recent excellent and thought-provoking books about altmetrics and alternative indicators (Holmberg, 2015; Cronin and Sugimoto, 2014), the focus of this book is on bringing together in one place the evidence, methods and tools needed to use web indicators in research evaluations.

As part of the goal to provide practical help, this book includes detailed instructions about how to use the free software Webometric Analyst to calculate simple and advanced indicators. This information is supplemented by the website hosting the software, which gives updates and additional help. The book does not attempt to be comprehensive in this regard and so does not explain how to process the free data provided by Altmetric.com to researchers, or how to calculate every possible indictor formula.

Chapters 1 to 7 and 11 target all readers, whereas the more technical Chapters 8 to 10 covering statistical and software issues are mainly designed for people who wish to collect their own web data and calculate a range of indicators from it. Chapter 9 on statistics is also useful for policy makers and research administrators. On a stylistic note, in places this book contains dense lists of correlation coefficients from different studies. These are usually restricted to paragraphs labelled "empirical evidence" and can be skipped on a first reading.

CHAPTER   2

Evaluating Indicators

Indicators must be evaluated before they can be used with any confidence. Evaluations can assess the type of impact represented by the indicator and the strength of the evidence that it provides. For example, while it may seem obvious that the public uses Twitter, and so counts of tweets about articles would be a useful indicator of public interest, this is usually not true (e.g., Thelwall et al., 2013b; but with some exceptions: Desai et al. 2012), and so tweet counts should not be used as indicators of public interest. Even the very general assumption that articles that are mentioned often in the social web tend to be more important needs supporting evidence. Web indicators also need to be evaluated because articles may be mentioned on the social web for negative reasons, such as to criticise them (Shema et al., 2012), to accuse the authors of fraud, to discuss retracted papers (Marcus and Oransky, 2011), for irrelevant reasons such as spam, or automated mentions (e.g., a journal tweeting all its articles, when published) or because they have funny or interesting titles. If alternative indicators are to be taken seriously in evaluations, then concrete evidence is needed to justify their use to those evaluated.

Some web indicators have an obvious face value interpretation, but these still need to be evaluated for evidence of bias and prevalence. An example is the online syllabus mention indicator. Unlike the case of tweet citations mentioned above, a citation from a course syllabus can be taken at face value as evidence of educational impact because course syllabi are created by instructors and the cited works contained in them are intended to be read by students as part of their education. Nevertheless, it is not immediately clear whether it would be fair to compare the educational impact of articles based on their online syllabus mentions because research can be used in education without being cited if it is summarised in standard course textbooks, part of a field that rarely recommends readings to students or included in syllabi that are not placed online. In addition, if very few course syllabi are posted to the public web then syllabus mention indictors would have too low coverage of academic research to have much practical value. A more general point is that a score of 0 on any particular indicator does not imply that the output assessed has had no impact, but only that no impact was recorded for it by the indicator.

For all of the above reasons, it is important to validate alternative indicators before use. Evaluations of indicators are not simple, however. Even citations, which are produced in a quality controlled environment (i.e., scholarly peer reviewed journals) and have been researched for decades, are controversial in two senses: whether they should be used at all (MacRoberts and MacRoberts, 1996; Seglen, 1998) and how their meaning should be interpreted (i.e., what they indicate) (Moed,

2005). The rest of this chapter discusses a range of accepted evaluation methods for indicators and makes overall recommendations for evaluation strategies.

The validation process is different from a common social sciences model of starting with a concept and then producing a series of measurements to capture it as well as possible (e.g., Lazarsfeld, 1958). The impact indicators discussed in this book (e.g., tweet citation counts) are instead essentially available before the concept rather than constructed to measure the concept. In consequence, the validation process needs to assess whether the indicator broadly reflects the type of impact that it appears to, as well as to find out in more detail about the type of impact, if any, that it represents.

A complicating issue is that it may be difficult to extract comprehensive data before calculating an indicator. The lack of a complete directory of blogs, for example, means that it is impossible to count all citations from blogs. It can also be difficult to extract accurate data. Counting the number of people who bookmarked an article online, for instance, may be difficult if some people maintain multiple social web bookmarking accounts and others share accounts. Indicators may also be systematically biased by marketing initiatives, such as authors, journals or institutions tweeting all of their articles. Most significantly, if an indicator becomes highly valued then authors, editors, or publishers may attempt to artificially inflate their scores. The lack of a quality control mechanism within the web makes deliberate and accidental manipulation difficult to stop.

2.1   EVALUATION METHODS

This section evaluates indicator data (e.g., tweet counts) rather than any specific indicator formula (e.g., median tweet counts). A range of methods has previously been used to investigate academic-related indicators. Correlation tests are the most common, but are insufficient on their own and particularly for web indicators that claim to reflect something other than scholarly impact.

2.1.1   HOW COMMON? COVERAGE ASSESSMENT

The prevalence of an indicator affects its usefulness; if a tiny fraction of articles received a non-zero count for a given indicator then it would have little value for applications that rely upon scores for individual articles, such as article altmetrics in a digital library. Nevertheless, low coverage does not preclude all applications because indicators with low coverage can still be used to compare the impact of groups of documents. This is possible by comparing the proportion that have a non-zero score between groups. For example, if group A had a higher proportion of articles with a non-zero score on a particular educational impact web indicator than group B then this would give some evidence of higher overall educational impact from group A. In general, the lower the coverage of the indicator, the larger the groups of articles that would need to be compared to detect differences between them.

2.1.2   CORRELATIONS WITH PEER REVIEW OR CITATION COUNTS

The most practical technique to help validate a research indicator is to calculate the correlation between it and a better understood data source, such as citation counts or peer review scores, even though these have their own biases (Lee et al., 2013; MacRoberts and MacRoberts, 1996; Wennerås and Wold, 1997). Correlations have been extensively used in webometrics to evaluate the evidence provided by links to journal websites or individual articles (Vaughan and Huysen, 2002; Vaughan and Shaw, 2003, 2005) or URL citations (Kousha and Thelwall, 2007) to articles or citations from various parts of the web (e.g., Thelwall and Kousha, 2008). They have also been introduced for altmetrics, playing a similar role (Li et al., 2012). Spearman correlations are normally used because citation data is typically too skewed for the normality assumption of a Pearson test. Given the relative trustworthiness of peer judgements, the best correlation would be between a rank order or scores produced by peer review and the rank order produced by the indicator. In practice it is difficult to get appropriate experts to rate lists of publications and so citation counts are routinely used instead on the basis that citations are an established research impact data source.

The rationale for calculating the correlation between an indicator and another source of research evidence (e.g., peer review rankings or citation scores) is that if they both reflect a type of research impact then the two rankings should be related, giving rise to a positive correlation coefficient, even if they reflect different types of research impact. In the hypothetical case that two indicators both measure pure research quality (assuming that this exists) then their correlation would always be positive, with a magnitude determined only by the amount of natural random fluctuations in the data. In the more realistic case that both partly reflect different aspects of research impact (e.g., educational utility or value for future scholarship) then the extent of the correlation would also depend upon how closely related these two aspects were. Finally, most metrics also probably reflect unwanted systematic causes of bias (e.g., institutional bias or time-dependency) which also affects the magnitude of a correlation and may even change its sign.

For web indicators, a positive correlation with citation counts gives evidence that the indicator at least partly reflects academic quality. This is because citation counts are known to partly reflect academic quality to some extent in most fields and so should correlate positively with any other indicator that also correlates with research quality. There is a gap in this logic because it is possible that citation counts and a web indicator have a positive correlation because they both reflect the same aspect of articles that is irrelevant to research quality, such as the publication language. Another gap is that the alternative indicator could have a zero correlation with citation counts because they both exclusively reflect completely different aspects of research quality. Nevertheless, these scenarios seem unlikely to occur in a pure form and so correlations with citation counts are an established test of association that is necessary to validate alternative indicators. A statistically significant positive correlation also gives evidence that the web indicator is not purely random. Thus, the positive correlation with citation counts in Figure 2.1 gives some evidence that Mendeley readers are valid research quality indicators for orthodontics articles and strong evidence that Mendeley readership data is not purely random.

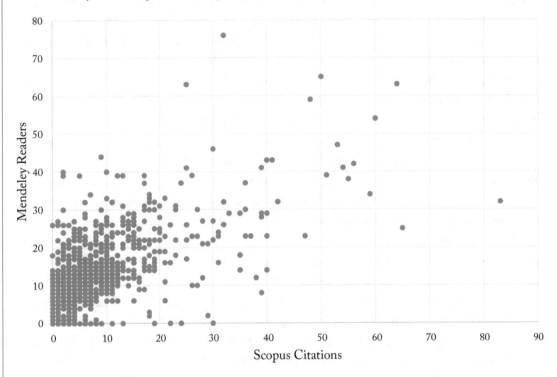

Figure 2.1: A scatter plot of Mendeley readers against Scopus citations for orthodontics articles from 2009. The graph shows a clear tendency for articles with many citations to also have many readers. A Spearman correlation of 0.744 reflects this strong relationship.

The potential for systematic causes of bias means that a positive correlation between a new and an established research indicator does not prove that the new indicator reflects an aspect of research quality because the correlation could be spurious and caused by a factor unrelated to research. Conversely, a negative correlation does not disprove the relationship because there may be an underlying research-related positive relationship that is suppressed by a factor unrelated to research. Hence, the onus is on the researcher to remove potential sources of bias as far as possible. For example, studies should focus on articles published within a limited time window to reduce the impact of time differences on the results. Collections of articles should also be as homogeneous as possible, such as by taking them all from the same journal or field and excluding reviews. In practice, positive correlations with citation counts are accepted as evidence of their value as indicators of an aspect of research impact if there is no obvious source of bias in the comparison made. The normal requirement for the test is that the correlation coefficient is statistically significant and greater than zero. Correlation calculations in scientometrics seem to always use several hundred articles or more, which is an adequate sample size.

The magnitude of a correlation coefficient is important, with higher values presenting stronger evidence of the value of the indicator as well as evidence that the relationship between the indicator and citation counts is closer. The strength of a correlation coefficient can be greatly reduced if the sets of articles being compared are from different fields or years (Thelwall, 2016d) and so articles should be separated out by field and year before calculating correlations. Low numbers and many zeros can also reduce correlation values, masking the strength of the underlying relationship (Thelwall, 2016d). Alternative indicators that increase rapidly within an individual year may need to be evaluated with the sign test (Section 9.10) rather than a correlation test because of this.

The main limitation of correlation tests between alternative indicators and citation counts is that they cannot give evidence of the *type* of impact reflected by the web indicator, if it is different from citation impact. Thus, if a new web indicator for educational impact is proposed then a positive correlation with citation counts demonstrates that it is not random and relates to scholarly activities in some way, but does not show whether it gives evidence of educational impact. Correlation tests alone are therefore insufficient for indicators that claim to reflect any non-scholarly type of impact.

2.1.3   WHY? CREATOR MOTIVATION INTERVIEWS OR QUESTIONNAIRES

The most direct way to assess whether an indicator reflects a particular type of impact is to interview the creators of the raw data (e.g., the tweeters for the tweet count altmetric) to find out why they created the data (e.g., a tweet). If the reasons tended to at least partially align with a particular type of impact, then this would support the validity of the indicator for that type of impact. For example, if most tweeters interviewed claimed to only tweet links to articles that they considered to be *useful* for research then it would be reasonable to claim tweet link counts as research utility indicators. In contrast, if most tweeters reported different motivations, such as tweeting articles with funny titles, then tweet counts could not be claimed to be research utility indicators.

In practice it is likely that a range of motivations would be elicited by interviews (Priem and Costello, 2010) and so in order for an indicator to be useful then the dominant reason(s) should relate to a specific type of impact (e.g., educational, commercial) and the other reasons should not introduce systematic sources of bias (i.e., common biases), unless they are too rare to be significant.

Creator motivation interviews have featured in few studies for three reasons: they are time consuming; they can only include a few relevant web authors; and authors may not be reliable because they have forgotten, do not understand or mask their reasons (as is the case for citations:

Brooks, 1986; Case and Higgins, 2000). Nevertheless, such interviews may give insights that are known only to the creators of the data and would not be evident from other methods. For example, interviews with tweeting academics revealed that some tweeted on the basis of reading blogs discussing articles rather than the articles themselves (Priem and Costello, 2010). The scope for future qualitative research of this nature seems limitless because of the range of indicators and likely differences in uptake and styles of use between researchers based upon countries, disciplines, fields and ages. What would be particularly useful in this regard, therefore, would be theories that would help to generalise patterns of use so that the inevitable large gaps in knowledge (e.g., for unexamined countries or disciplines) would not cause problems. A corollary to this is that contextual information about the value of indicators from creator interviews or questionnaires is likely to always be patchy in terms of the fields and indicators investigated.

Creator motivation questionnaires are also rare partly because it is usually difficult to get a representative sample of creators. One exception used an elaborate process to get the email addresses of a large sample of Mendeley users (Mohammadi et al., 2016) in order to send them a questionnaire asking how and why they employed the service.

2.1.4   WHY? SOURCE CONTENT ANALYSIS

A practical alternative to author interviews or questionnaires is to conduct a content analysis of a random sample of raw data (e.g., tweets with citations) to categorise the contexts or the apparent citation motivations (Priem and Costello, 2010). This is non-intrusive, can be conducted on a larger scale than interviews or questionnaires, and does not rely upon author memories. Its disadvantages are that insufficient context may be available for a reliable classification in some cases, coders may be fooled by clever spam and it is labour-intensive to do well. The amount of context and hence the usefulness of this approach varies by data source. While tweets may be too short, blog posts should typically give enough context for reliable coding. Any content analysis should follow standard guidelines: using careful descriptions and multiple coders and reporting inter-coder reliability (Neuendorf, 2002).

Content analyses have been rarely used for alternative indicators (exceptions: Priem and Costello, 2010; Thelwall et al., 2013b) but deserve to be more common. In addition to giving evidence about why the raw data was created, which is essential to validate the type of impact reflected by indicators, they can improve the wider understanding of their meaning by revealing their typical contexts.

As for interviews, in order for a content analysis to provide evidence of research value in the associated indicator, the dominant (not necessarily the majority) category should be related to the type of impact claimed and the remainder should not introduce systematic sources of bias, unless they are much smaller. These provisos greatly complicate the interpretation of the results: unless reasons related to a single impact type are in an overwhelming majority, a qualitative argument must be made for the remaining categories not introducing systematic biases.

2.1.5   WHO? CREATOR TYPE QUESTIONNAIRES AND DATA

In addition to finding out *why* indicator values are created, it is also important to know who creates them. For example, it would be useful to know who uses the social web for scholarly purposes and which parts they use (Weller et al., 2010; Procter et al., 2010). This information can point to systematic biases, such as towards younger users or females. This can be investigated using questionnaires, with the same considerations as above.

The demographics of the creators of indicator data can also sometimes be investigated directly from the source by extracting information about them from the web. In one study, properties of Mendeley readers (e.g., academic status and nationality) were harvested from the Mendeley.com API in order to give large-scale information (Mohammadi et al., 2015).

2.1.6   PRAGMATIC EVALUATIONS

A final type of evaluation is pragmatic (Helic et al., 2011): testing whether a specific use of an indicator helps to achieve a desired goal. In other words, this means evaluating the use of the indicator in practice. In research assessments a pragmatic evaluation would involve discovering the opinions of some or all of the participants about their perceptions of the usefulness of the indicators provided. Depending upon the scale of the evaluations, this could take the form of interviews or questionnaires. Assessors could be asked whether they felt that the indicators helped them to arrive at a more accurate or quicker judgement. Such assessments were conducted informally for the UK REF2014 assessment to discover which disciplines found citation counts to be useful indicators. Similar sessions do not seem to have been conducted yet for any alternative indicator. For indicators displayed on a publisher's website, a pragmatic evaluation might instead ask users whether they believed that altmetrics helped them to find important or useful articles.

2.2   DELIBERATE AND ACCIDENTAL MANIPULATION OF RESULTS

A problem that affects typical web indicators is that they can be manipulated due to a lack of quality control. Accidental manipulation might occur, for example, though publicity for articles by their authors and publishing journals. Assuming that accidental manipulation of this type is ongoing at a constant level, the techniques discussed in the previous section should be adequate to assess whether it is substantial enough to affect a given indicator. The question here is not whether accidental manipulation occurs but whether it is common and systematic enough to substantially alter the meaning of a given indicator.

A more problematic issue is the deliberate manipulation that may occur if alternative indicators are used to assess researchers when the researchers know about the choice of indicators in advance and have an interest in a positive outcome (Wouters and Costas, 2012). It is difficult to empirically evaluate the extent to which this is a problem for an indicator but it seems reasonable to assume that a web indictor will be deliberately manipulated whenever it can be. Although web indicators all fail this test, they can still be used for other types of evaluations. Also, if the evaluations are not of a high value nature, then it may be possible to employ strategies to reduce the likelihood of manipulation, such as honesty clauses or a degree of random or automatic checking of the data for signs of manipulation (e.g., Zimmermann, 2013).

2.3   SUMMARY AND RECOMMENDATIONS

The methods described in this chapter (correlation tests, creator interviews, or questionnaires, source content analysis and pragmatic evaluations) can all give evidence about the value or meaning of new indicators. While all of the methods have limitations, these can be at least partially overcome by using multiple different types (method triangulation). The following strategy is recommended for researchers seeking to evaluate any alternative indicator, based upon the above discussion.

1. Coverage analysis to assess the proportion of documents that have a non-zero score for the indicator. Low coverage restricts the number of practical applications of the indicator. In practice, coverage analyses are often conducted in parallel with correlation tests.

2. Correlations between the indicator and citation counts for diverse sets of individual fields and years to identify when they are likely to work. This is the simplest test to apply on a large scale and so is the first step. This also addresses the issue of whether the indicator works at all, but does not give evidence about the type of impact reflected by the indicator, if different from research impact. For this, at least one of the approaches below is needed unless the impact type is obvious.

3. Content analyses of selected sources of the indicator to find out why they were created. These are a logical next step because of the likely greater coverage in comparison to interviews and greater simplicity in comparison to surveys. The results will help to validate a claim for the type of impact that they may reflect (e.g., societal and educational). In addition, the results can help to give a finer-grained interpretation of the meaning of the indicator. Content analyses are not possible for usage indicators, which do not provide qualitative context.

4. Creator motivation surveys to find out why the data was created.

5. Creator motivation interviews on a small scale for detailed insights into potentially unknown reasons why indicator values were created.

6. User interviews, surveys or data analyses to understand what types of people create the indicator data and how they differ from typical academics (e.g., younger, more likely to work in industry).

7. Pragmatic evaluations to assess the use of indicators in practice. These are the logical final step but may be conducted in advance by organisations that conduct trials with the indicator, such as publishers, and are primarily concerned with user opinions.

For people using alternative indicators but not evaluating them, the most important lesson from this chapter is that while statistically significant positive correlations between an alternative indicator and citation counts provide the most common source of evidence for their use, this alone is insufficient to assess the type of impact reflected or to validate a claim that they reflect a specific type of non-scholarly impact.

CHAPTER 3

Usage, Popularity and Attention Indicators

An important indication of the level of interest in an academic output is the number of times that it has been used (Kurtz and Bollen, 2010). While documents are read and videos are watched, data and software may be downloaded and processed or enhanced. Usage data for documents may take different forms, including digital library downloads, online views, book sales and library holdings. It is also possible to refer to an artefact without necessarily using it. For example, librarians might tweet links to relevant articles without necessarily reading them. An attention indicator records how often an artefact has been noticed on a particular website, such as Twitter.

At the most basic level, an artefact must be used to be appreciated and so things that are rarely noticed are unlikely to have value. Usage indicators like view or download counts can therefore give important basic knowledge although they may give no insights into how something was used. It is difficult to give a concrete interpretation of many usage indicators in practice because of a lack of contextual information but the hypothesis that something must be used to be useful can still allow them to serve as impact indicators. The same is true for attention indicators and so these are the most general indicators in the sense that they do not suggest a type of impact. Nevertheless, in some cases it may be possible to infer a type of impact from the context. For example, if usage data is available for a set of educational textbooks then it would be reasonable to interpret this as educational impact evidence. Thus, all of the indicators discussed in this chapter could fit in the other chapters on more specific impact types for some applications. In particular, since the main audience for the work of scholars is other scholars, a usage indicator for most academic outputs is also likely to be a type of academic impact indicator.

Popularity indicators, such as like counts, give a little more information because they report the extent to which something has been appreciated but still do not give information about the impact type.

3.1 GENERAL WEB CITATIONS

Counting the number of times that an article has been cited or mentioned online can, in theory, give an overall indicator of the level of interest in it. Although such a figure would encompass many different reasons for invoking the article, an overall level of interest indicator might still be useful.

It is possible to use a search engine to retrieve pages citing an article by querying for key article metadata, such as the title in quotes, together with the first author last name, journal title and publication year. This information is normally enough to ensure a correct citation unless the article has a short title. For example, the following Google query has been constructed to find web citations to a document.

```
"Decrease in Net Stool Output in Cholera during In-
testinal Perfusion with Glucose-Containing Solutions"
"New England Journal of Medicine" Hirschhorn 1968
```

The above query is likely to get only correct matches to the (seminal) article: *Hirschhorn, Norbert; Kinzie, Joseph L.; Sachar, David B.; Northrup, Robert S.; Taylor, James O.; Ahmad, S. Zafar; Phillips, Robert A. (1968). "Decrease in Net Stool Output in Cholera during Intestinal Perfusion with Glucose-Containing Solutions." New England Journal of Medicine 279 (4): 176–81. doi:10.1056/NEJM196807252790402*. In contrast, articles with short titles may get some incorrect results, as in the following case, and the problem is particularly acute for articles with short titles in journals with short names, such as *Nature, Science,* and *Cell*.

```
"Red, white and blue" "Word Ways" Ashley 1979
```

The above query generates some false matches for the article: *Ashley, L. R. N. (1979). Red, white and blue, Word Ways, 12(3), article 18.* With a few exceptions it is therefore possible to use queries like the above to count web citations to academic articles. This counting can be done with the normal Google search interface for a few articles. For large collections, the process can be automated by constructing and submitting the queries with the free Webometric Analyst software (see Chapter 8). Articles with short titles may need to be excluded or their results manually filtered, if practical, in order to obtain a set of reasonably accurate results.

General web citations are attractive for their ability to incorporate varied types of use of articles but their main problem for journal articles is the number of trivial matches. For example, these occur in the journal tables of contents that are frequently listed on the web by publishers and libraries for recording and publicity purposes. In addition, publications may be listed on the author's online CV. In practice, therefore, the web citation method is most useful for papers that have not been published in serials and that are not subject to systematic publicity. This excludes most papers and books released by official publishers. Nevertheless, general web citations may be useful for informally published documents, such as white papers, research reports, government reports, policy briefings: the grey literature. For example, it might be informative to count the general web citations of all the policy briefings produced by an organisation and its own publicity could be excluded from the results by removing all matches from its website. For example, to search for web citations to the policy briefing *Nesta Ideas Bank: Ideas to Transform Scotland*, the following query would exclude all matches from the website of its creator, Nesta, www.nesta.org.uk,

```
"Nesta Ideas Bank: ideas to transform Scotland"
-site:nesta.org.uk
```

This is because the site: keyword in Google and Bing matches pages within a website. Adding a minus sign before it excludes pages from that site. The results of the above query should therefore be web citations to the briefing from anywhere on the web except Nesta's website (Figure 3.1).

"Nesta Ideas Bank: ideas to transform Scotland" -site:ne

Web   Images   Videos   Maps   News   Explore

9 RESULTS   Date ▾   Language ▾   Region ▾

NESTA ideas bank: ideas to transform Scotland
kingsfund.blogs.com/health_management/2016/05/nesta-ideas-bank... ▾
NESTA - This report discusses innovative policy solutions to transform **Scotland's** health and care system, democratic process and creative industries.

NHS Evidence - **health management** | Healthcare People ...
www.hpma.org.uk/aggregator/sources/8?page=5 ▾
NESTA ideas bank: ideas to transform Scotland. Mon, 09/05/2016 - 10:29. NESTA - ...

Figure 3.1: A Bing search for webpages mentioning the report *Nesta Ideas Bank: Ideas to Transform Scotland*, showing the first two results.

Coverage: Although there are no recent studies, it seems likely that almost all academic books and journal articles are mentioned online, giving coverage close to 100%.

Empirical evidence: While early pioneering research found that web citations to academic articles tended to have positive correlations with traditional citations to them, many of the web citations originated from journal tables of contents and library website listings, undermining the value of web citations in practice (Vaughan and Shaw, 2003, 2005). A technical alternative to the web citation is the URL citation, which is a mention of the URL of an article rather than its title. URL citations give similar results to web citations but have the disadvantage that few web citations to articles include a URL and so their coverage is lower (Kousha and Thelwall, 2007).

Interpretation: Because web citations can be created for many reasons, the results can only be interpreted in very general terms. Web citation counts should therefore be viewed as attention indicators. In specific cases the citations may be for a relatively narrow set of reasons but systematic evidence of this would be needed, such as from a content analysis exercise, if a more specific type of impact than attention or interest is claimed.

3.2   ARTICLE DOWNLOAD AND VIEW COUNTS

It is impossible to be sure how often an article has been read because reading does not leave a recordable trace. Nevertheless, some activities associated with reading do leave a record, such as downloading an article from the publisher's or author's website or visiting a webpage containing it. Counting article downloads gives an imperfect measure of readership because someone might decide not to read an article after downloading it and examining its abstract. Others might read an article without accessing it electronically because they subscribe to a print version of the journal, read it in a library, or were given a printout by their lecturer. Some may even access an illegal copy of the article in an untraceable way.

On a small scale, download statistics may be identified for individual articles from their pages within the publisher's website, if it reports this information. Unfortunately, there are technical problems with such figures. Some article downloads may be from web crawlers or other automated processes that do not reflect human readers. People may also download an article multiple times despite reading it only once. This may occur by accident or as a result of not saving a local copy and needing to check a document several times. Crawlers and multiple accesses may be automatically excluded from download count data if the publisher has software to do this. Conversely, an unscrupulous publisher may artificially inflate download counts to make their journals appear to be more popular. These issues have led to the COUNTER agreement between publishers to exercise a similar level of care with their download statistics (www.projectcounter.org). COUNTER-compliant article download counts therefore seem more likely to be accurate than others. Nevertheless, it is impossible to filter out administrative accesses of articles—such as by authors and research administrators seeking to recover copies of their articles or to check their metadata.

Institutional and subject-based repositories are additional sources of download statistics. In some fields, such as Physics, it is common practice to deposit preprints in the main subject repository (arXiv.org for physics, computing and related quantitative fields). Download statistics from such repositories may be more valuable than, or similarly valuable to, data from publishers. They are unlikely to be comparable between repositories, however, and arXiv deliberately does not provide any. RePEc (Research Papers in Economics), in contrast, provides citation and download statistics for its papers and includes substantial automated and manual checking for download spamming (Zimmermann, 2013). This spam filtering is important because the statistics are used for league tables on the site and there have been attempts to manipulate them. The presence of a subject repository can give relatively easy access to comparable download data for the entire field, avoiding the problem of publishers following different standards. Articles are likely to attract a varying proportion of their downloads from the repository, depending on the topic of the paper, because multidisciplinary articles may attract readers from other fields that do not use the archive. Journal open access policies will also affect the level of downloading of articles from a repository.

Coverage: Almost all online academic artefacts will presumably have been accessed at least once by their author, giving coverage close to 100%. In practice, however, the main coverage issues are whether the artefact is available in an electronic version (some books are not) and whether download or view count statistics are available for those that are online.

Empirical evidence: Article downloads tend to have a positive correlation with citation counts in many but not all fields. An early study found that the number of downloads of an article in the NASA Astrophysics Data System was a good indicator for its future citation count (Kurtz et al., 2005; for a follow-up see: Kurtz and Henneken, in press). This relationship has been confirmed by a subsequent study of the subject repository arXiv, finding that the correlation between downloads (within arXiv) and citations rose to 0.432 after two years (Brody et al., 2006). These investigations might represent special cases where there is a single dominant source of downloads for a field, whereas in other subject areas there are more varied article sources. A later large-scale comparison of download counts from Elsevier's ScienceDirect with peer review scores for articles from 2008 submitted to the 2014 UK REF found correlations varying from -0.593 for Chemistry (n=120) to 0.423 for Public Health (n=200) and 0.440 for Philosophy (n=15). Just over half (18 out of 32) of the correlations were positive (HEFCE, 2015). The mixed results here are probably due to readers accessing the papers from multiple different sources: subject and institutional repositories, author pages, academic social websites and publisher websites. Aggregating articles by journal, the correlation between ScienceDirect downloads and Scopus citations is about 0.3 in the arts and humanities, 0.5 in social science, 0.65 in natural sciences and engineering and 0.8 in medicine (Halevi and Moed, 2014). This study suggests that at the individual article level the overall Spearman correlation between Scopus citations and ScienceDirect downloads is about 0.9 (from a visual inspection of Figure 7 in Halevi and Moed, 2014).

Interpretation: It seems reasonable to interpret article download and view counts as rough evidence of overall readership, despite the limitations discussed above. This indicator is likely to be more accurate when there is a single primary source for articles, such as if the journal is online only, does not allow authors to post preprints elsewhere and filters download statistics carefully. In terms of the type of impact, readers of scientific articles seem likely to be mainly scholars, and this supposition is supported by the relatively high correlations found with citation counts, as discussed above. Nevertheless, professionals and students also read articles and so article accesses may reflect a combination of academic, educational and professional impacts, with the exact combination depending on the field. Thus, while the most appropriate generic description for download or view counts is usage indicators, in fields where articles are rarely read by non-academics, such as some pure maths topics, it may be clear that they are academic impact indictors.

3.3   RESEARCHGATE AND ACADEMIA.EDU DOWNLOAD AND VIEW COUNTS

Academic social network sites like ResearchGate and Academia.edu allow researchers to create profiles that include prominent lists of their publications, with the option to upload full text versions of these publications. ResearchGate had, at least in 2014, a particularly large pool of regular academic users, just short of Google Scholar in this regard but ahead of LinkedIn, Academia.edu and Twitter (Van Noorden, 2014). ResearchGate and Academia.edu record and display counts of the number of times that each article has been downloaded (if available in full text) or its metadata viewed. This gives a new source of usage data. If these sites have substantial numbers of users, then they will undermine usage data from publishers by providing an alternative source of articles. If the view or download counts in these sites are extracted for indicators, then they have the limitation that the users of these sites are likely to be a biased subset of all article readers. This bias is likely to be towards younger and more technologically competent readers. There are also likely to be international biases in the uptake of each site that may transfer into biases in patterns of reading. An additional problem is that the statistics seem to be easily spammed.

Academic social network sites organise researchers by institutional affiliation and ResearchGate (currently) provides ranked lists of universities based on the combined properties of researchers on the site. These rankings are clearly influenced by the extent to which members of a university have signed up to the site. The ranked lists of scores based on activity within the sites are not relevant for academic indicators.

It is possible to score academics based on their activities within academic social network sites and this might provide indicators of ways in which scholars can contribute to the community other than through publication (Hoffmann et al., 2015).

Coverage: All articles on ResearchGate seem to have been viewed at least once (Thelwall and Kousha, in press-a) and the same is probably true for Academia.edu, but the coverage of these sites in terms of the proportion of WoS or Scopus articles in them is unknown.

Empirical evidence: Rankings of institutions based on ResearchGate data correlate positively with other academic institutional rankings (Thelwall and Kousha, 2015; Yu et al., 2016). View counts for articles in ResearchGate seem to have low positive correlations with citation counts that vary by field. For articles uploaded to ResearchGate in July 2014 and published before 2004, correlations with citations varied from 0.28 (medicine, agriculture) to 0.45 (biochemistry), although only five fields were checked (Thelwall and Kousha, in press-a). There does not seem to be any empirical evidence about article views on Academia.edu, probably because these are not downloadable with a standard web crawler.

Interpretation: View and download counts on academic social websites can be interpreted as evidence of readership, but their potential biases should be acknowledged. As for other sources of article downloads and views, the default description should be as a usage indicator, but in some contexts a more specific impact type may be appropriate.

3.4   VIEW, ACCESS OR DOWNLOAD COUNTS FOR OTHER SCHOLARLY OUTPUTS

Most of the above discussion also applies to other scholarly outputs: it can be useful to count how often they have been viewed, accessed or downloaded as an imperfect indicator of how often they have been used. For things other than journal articles, the likelihood of irrelevant downloads is probably higher, because many websites may not be careful with their view, download or access counts and may allow practices that artificially inflate them. A particular problem with non-standard scholarly outputs is that the size of their intended audience may vary greatly and so it may not be reasonable to compare view access or download counts between resources. For example, one researcher might create videos aimed at school children that get 1,000 views each and another might create a video for other researchers describing how to conduct an experiment with a complex apparatus and attract only 10 views. It is not clear that these 10 views by scientists are worth less than the 1,000 views by pupils, because the former might provide irreplaceable and substantial help to the scientists with their goals, whereas the children might be entertained but only slightly informed by the video. The following are some important types of non-scholarly outputs for which it could be useful to count views, accesses or downloads.

Computer software can substantially benefit researchers and others if the source code is shared online in a bespoke open source software repository, such as GitHub.com, or if the compiled program is deposited online, such as in the academic resource-sharing site FigShare (e.g., the popular program igraph: Csardi and Nepusz, 2006). Counts of downloads of the software or code can provide evidence about the size of its user base. These figures could be underestimates if the code is incorporated into other programs, so that users downloading the new software benefit from the recycled code without needing to download the original. Download counts should not be routinely compared between different programs because even relatively trivial computing contributions can sometimes fill a wide need and attract high download counts—as is the case for one collection of icons (Thelwall and Kousha, 2016a). The fundamental reason is that computer programs are used for such a wide variety of purposes that they are not easily comparable when they do not attempt to solve the same problem.

Research data sharing is important in some areas and there are a number of specific data sharing repositories, such as Dryad (Miller, 2016), for this. General purpose academic resource sharing repositories like FigShare can also be used successfully to share data (Thelwall and Kousha, 2016b). Counting data downloads can give an idea of the level of interest in it but the uses are likely to vary greatly in depth. For example, one download may lead to an important new paper whereas another might be used by a student for a class project.

Images sharing is important in astronomy and the arts, where it can help to engage the public in topics of academic interest. Image search engines can be used to count how often individual images have been replicated online to serve as a usage indicator (Kousha et al., 2010b).

Videos shared online and created by academics may be used for science outreach, for education, to describe their work, or may be the main outputs of some scholars. The most popular science outreach site is currently the TED Talks website that hosts thousands of curated talks by academics and others. Since these talks all target a wide audience it would be reasonable to compare the view counts for videos uploaded (Sugimoto and Thelwall, 2013). Any comparisons should be made at a similar point in time to avoid giving an unfair advantage to older videos. In contrast, videos uploaded to SlideShare could have any target audience and so it would be difficult to justify comparing view counts between them. This is even more true for academic videos on YouTube because the huge user base of the site and its overall recreational focus gives the potential for videos to be watched casually for purposes other than that for which they were intended. Nevertheless, an academic who had created a successful video could use its YouTube or SlideShare view count as evidence of its success as long as they set the figures in context with the purpose of the video and acknowledged that it may have been used for other purposes. For example, the very high view count of the "Lady Gaga's 'Bad Romance' played on the Iowa State University carillon" video (over 800,000 views by July 2016: Figure 3.2) is good evidence that the music and theatre scholar Tin-Shi Tam has created something that triggered wide public interest.

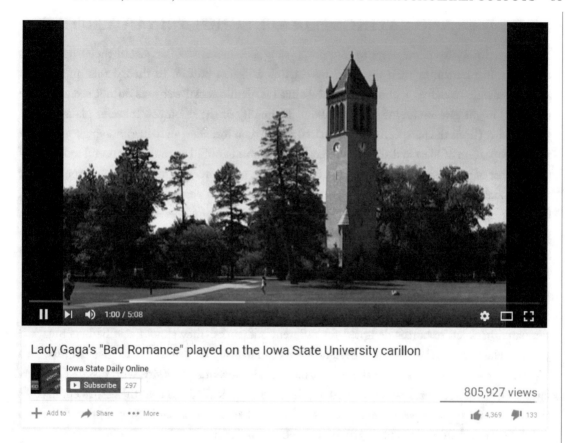

Figure 3.2: A YouTube video produced by an academic, showing the number of views underneath.

Coverage: Most online academic outputs are likely to have been viewed, accessed and downloaded at least once by their creator, giving coverage close to 100%.

Empirical evidence: Download counts for projects in Google Code have a weak correlation (0.27) with their Scopus citations (Thelwall and Kousha, 2016a). Papers which share their data tend to attract more citations (Piwowar et al., 2007), which supports the value of data re-use. Empirical evidence does not seem to be available yet for the other sources discussed.

Interpretation: The type of impact generated by non-standard scholarly outputs is the most complex to discuss. For all types of resources, the nature of their impact is very context specific and the impact type of these indicators can only be expressed with the very general term usage impact, even though for specific types of resource the intended use may be clear and a narrower impact type may be assumed (e.g., educational, academic).

3.5 LIKES AND RATINGS FOR ALL SCHOLARLY OUTPUTS

Many social websites allow users to rate posts using a standard scale or record their approval by clicking a like button or their disproval by clicking a dislike button. In theory, this information about academic resources within general websites (academic social websites do not seem to have these yet) might give useful information about the quality of the resources. It seems plausible that good quality (from the perspective of the actual rather than intended audience) resources would get a high proportion of likes to dislikes and that the total number of likes could be a useful indicator of the number of people who found it useful. Nevertheless, a resource might be liked for aspects other than its quality, such as if it had a funny title or if it presented a perspective that the viewer agreed with. For example, videos about religion or politics may get many likes and dislikes from partisan viewers irrespective of the quality of the video or argument. Likes are rarely used for academic-related indicators but one exception is an analysis of videos from the TED website (Sugimoto and Thelwall, 2013). Ratings have been used in book-based evaluations, however.

As with usage metrics, rating and counts (or the ratio of likes to dislikes, or the proportion of resource accesses that trigger a like) have context-specific interpretations and should not be compared between resources designed for different audiences. They should also be benchmarked against values for similar resources designed for a similar audience in order to give context. This is particularly important because there is probably a bias towards positivity, with dissatisfied users forgetting about a resource rather than taking the time to click Dislike. Nevertheless, except in cases of controversial topics, it seems reasonable to interpret like counts as an indicator of usefulness to the audience and stronger than an attention or access indicator.

Coverage: Coverage is likely to vary widely by site.

Empirical evidence: There seems to be no empirical evidence of the value of like counts for academic content. Ratings of books in Amazon have a low positive Spearman correlation with their Scopus citation counts. The coefficient is 0.2 in the social sciences, arts and humanities and 0.1 in science (including book citations) (Kousha and Thelwall, 2016a).

Interpretation: Likes and ratings reflect usage or popularity but a more specific impact type would be appropriate if the documents or resources assessed have a known audience type, such as scholars, professionals or students.

3.6 CITATIONS AND LINKS FROM TWITTER AND WEIBO

Twitter and Weibo are prominent general purpose microblogging sites that allow users to broadcast short public messages. These posts may embed links or contain citations to academic outputs (Figure 3.3). They are publicly searchable so that any web user could read them and posts are injected into the news streams of the post author's followers, giving them a ready audience.

Mike Thelwall @mikethelwall · May 9
Too many uncited articles? Zero inflated variants of the discretised lognormal and hooked power law distributions
authors.elsevier.com/a/1S-1U6EAije3...

Figure 3.3: A tweet about a research article including a link to access the article.

Microblogs seem to be mainly used for discussing general or personal news with a focus on events that have just happened. Their ostensible purpose is not to create authoritative content or a public record but to discuss current happenings. For example, Twitter asks its users to tweet about what they are doing now. Weibo is a China-focused microblog site that is more popular than Twitter in China but that has similar properties and perhaps also similar patterns of use. Twitter (ranked 8 globally by Alexa in June 2016: http://www.alexa.com/topsites) and Weibo (ranked 21 globally and 5 in China by Alexa in June 2016) are both extremely popular sites and so it is logical to assess whether their posts could be harvested for indicators of popular interest in scientific articles.

Do microblog posts reflect public interest in academic research? Although most microblog users are not academics, the vast majority of posts about research are probably written by scholars or computer programs. One content analysis of a sample of tweets linking to academic articles found no evidence of posts from non-academics (Thelwall et al., 2013b). This dominance can occur because academics are naturally much more interested in research than the public and are the primary audience for most academic publications. In addition, a substantial number of academic outputs are not understandable to a lay audience, and non-scholars rarely have a tradition of citing primary sources of evidence. Thus, even though microblogs could in theory give evidence of wider public interest in academic research, they mainly reflect academic interest except in exceptional circumstances. The most prolific academic tweeters may not be the same as the most prolific authors (Haustein et al., 2014a) and so it seems likely that many academic tweets are not from the authors of the tweeted work. Substantial numbers of tweets about scholarly articles are also generated by automatic agents, either tweeting about a common topic or tweeting all articles from a particular website, such as arXiv.org or publisher digital libraries (Haustein et al., 2016). Thus, tweets about research also reflect publicity to some extent.

A second issue to consider when interpreting the number of microblog posts about an article is that there are many reasons why someone might want to post about academic research. From an indicator perspective, the ideal motivation might be that someone has read an article, found it to be interesting and useful, and then posted about it to share their discovery with others in their network. If all tweets were created like this, then counting posts would give an indicator of academic research quality. In contrast, an irrelevant motivation occurs when the author, publisher or journal editor promotes an article by tweeting about it. This is presumably common and so publicity is an important motivation for tweeting about research. There are also relatively trivial reasons for tweeting articles that derive from microblogs being on social media and scientists occasionally engaging in purely social communication. An article might be tweeted to generate amusement if its title or content was perceived to be entertaining (e.g., the 16th highest score in Altmetric.com in 2015 was for the 2014 article, "Shaping the oral microbiota through intimate kissing," which had a modest citation count of 21 in Google Scholar by June 2016: https://www.altmetric.com/top100/2015/). Someone might also tweet their friends' articles or the new work of well-known scholars. Despite the use of Twitter for publicity and entertainment, tweet counts can still be research quality *indicators* if they tend to associate with research quality.

Another limitation is that not all social web posts convey the same weight of evidence in the sense that some are composed after careful consideration by experts whereas others are generated by a single casual button click. Assuming that automatically generated posts created by robots can be filtered out, the single button click tweets are particularly problematic. These legitimately occur in article webpages within some publishers' websites. Such a page may have a pre-composed but customisable relevant post (e.g., the article title and a link to the article page) and only a single click would be needed to send it as a Tweet, Weibo, Facebook or Reddit post from a user's personal account, assuming that they were already logged in. This facility presumably ensures that a much higher proportion of article readers post about articles from social media–friendly publishers than from others. Thus, any comparison of counts of posts between articles from different publishers may be misleading.

A technical issue with identifying citations from microblogs is that posts tend to be too short to contain a full citation in addition to a moderate amount of associated text. Microbloggers may instead cite articles by linking to a relevant page, such as an online preprint or the article page within the journal website. They may also give a DOI or an oblique reference, such as "Smith's latest paper just published in JASIST." Any counts of citations from a microblog site therefore depend on the methods used to extract citations.

Coverage: Although there is no evidence about academic books, more articles have tweet citations than any other type of social web mentions, at least in the data collected by Altmetric. com (Costas et al., 2015b; Thelwall et al., 2013a). Almost half (49%) of articles published in the general journal *PLOS One* in 2013 had been tweeted by 2014 (Zahedi et al., 2014a) and 70% of recent articles from 785 high-impact science journals had been tweeted at least once (Alhoori and Furuta, 2014). As is the case for all web indicators examined, coverage is much weaker for national literatures. For example, only 2% of Latin American journal articles from 2013 had been tweeted by 2014 (Alperin, 2015).

Empirical evidence: The first empirical study of Tweets as an impact metric found evidence that tweet counts could be used to predict future citations with a success rate better than random guessing (Eysenbach, 2011), but the evidence was presented for one high profile online journal and the same may not be true for others (see also: Shuai et al., 2012). Another early study found no correlation between tweets and citations, attributing this to the rapidly increasing uptake of Twitter (at the time), with people tending to tweet just-published articles. Because of this, newer articles tended to be more tweeted. In contrast, older articles had longer to be cited and so tended to have higher citation counts (Thelwall et al., 2013a). A later study of PubMed articles found statistically significant but low positive correlations between citation counts and tweet counts for articles from individual disciplines and years, averaging 0.157, but varying between -0.645 for arts (n=71) and -0.209 for mathematics (n=2461) to 0.232 for biomedical research (n=286,398) (Haustein et al., 2014b). An analysis of WoS publications from multiple categories found an overall low correlation of 0.167 (Costas et al., 2015b). Surprisingly, in this context, counts of tweets to articles (from the year 2008) have a (low) positive correlation with peer review judgements of the quality of the articles in 30 out of 36 broad subject areas, with the highest value being 0.234 (for art and design, n=130), using UK Research Excellence Framework 2014 data (HEFCE, 2015). The correlations tend to be very low, with 22 of the 30 positive correlations being less than 0.1. Overall, then, tweet counts tend to have a low correlation with citation counts and peer review scores. This low value suggests that tweets partly reflect the quality or impact of the tweeted articles and partly reflect other factors, such as the volume of publicity for them and social tweeting factors. There does not appear to be any similar empirical evidence about the value of Sina Weibo or other microblogging sites and so the default position should be that they are also likely to provide weak impact evidence.

Interpretation: Although there is no specific empirical evidence to support this claim, the most reasonable interpretation of microblog posts count is as an interest or attention indicator. As an indicator rather than a direct measure, the existence of irrelevant motivations, such as publicity or social reasons, does not invalidate this claim since there are more substantial motivations. It also seems likely that some users post about articles that look interesting and topically relevant without necessarily reading and evaluating them first.

3.6.1   REPOSTS

An important feature of microblogs is that users can forward others' posts, for example by retweeting. Retweet counts can be used as attention indicators for individual tweets and can be used as evidence of the success or reach of individual tweets but they do not seem to be used as an academic indicator. Their use as an indicator for articles would be possible if the number of retweets of the original author or publisher publicity tweet was counted. This does not make sense, however, because an article can easily be tweeted about without retweeting the publisher's tweet. In contrast, if an article is tweeted about by anyone then it would be possible to include all retweets within the count the number of times that the article had been tweeted. This is undesirable from the perspective that it takes more effort to compose a new tweet than to retweet an existing one. Similarly, although some original tweets are generated by button clicks on publisher websites, such button clicks at least indicate that the user has taken the time to visit the page of the article, which is not necessarily true for retweeters. An ideal solution would be to weight a retweet at a fraction of the value of an original tweet, using empirical evidence to identify the most appropriate fraction to use but this does not seem to have been done yet.

3.7   CITATIONS IN GENERAL SOCIAL NETWORK SITES: FACEBOOK, GOOGLE+

Social network sites are websites that allow users to join, normally without charge, to have a public profile, and to publicly connect with other members. These public connections take the form of public lists of Friends, subscribers, or followers. The most prominent current example of a social network site is Facebook but some countries have more popular variants, such as Vk.com in Russia. Many microblogging sites, such as Twitter and Sina Weibo, are also social network sites, as are many resource-oriented social websites, including YouTube and Flickr. The focus in this section is on general social network sites rather than those that specialise in microblogging, videos or any other type of resource.

General social network sites often incorporate a microblog in the form of public messages posted on user profile pages. In Facebook these are currently called wall posts. As in Twitter, such posts can target individuals but are, by default, broadcast instead. These posts may occasionally discuss academic research and so have the same potential to be harnessed for indicators as microblog posts. The main difference is that general social network sites are not mainly designed for news exchange in the way that microblogs are and so it seems likely that they will provide fewer posts per user. A practical disadvantage is that general social network site posts might be private by default for a large fraction of users, which reduces the amount of data available for indicators.

Coverage: About 21% of recent articles from 785 high impact science journals had been cited in Facebook and 4% in Google+ according to altmetric.com data (Alhoori and Furuta, 2014). The figure for general articles is probably substantially below 18%, however (see Table 3 in: Thelwall et al., 2013a). Only 0.6% of Latin American journal articles from 2013 had been cited by Facebook wall posts by 2014 according to Altmetric.com data (Alperin, 2015).

Empirical evidence: The number of Facebook or Google Plus posts mentioning academic articles, as gathered by Altmetric.com has been shown to have a very small positive correlation with citation counts and to be much rarer than tweets (Costas et al., 2015b; Thelwall et al., 2013a).

Interpretation: As in the case of posts from microblog sites, it seems reasonable to characterise counts of citations from general social network sites as indicators of interest and attention. It seems likely that author publicity would exist in any general social network site in which academic research is often cited, and this will probably reduce the overall strength of indicators.

3.8   BOOK REVIEW COUNTS AND RATINGS

Although book reviews published in academic journals (e.g., Champion and Morris, 1973) are a recognised source of impact evidence for scholarly monographs, there are new large-scale web-based sources of book reviews that may provide evidence of the reception of books by non-academics. The Choice website systematically reviews all types of books from the perspective of librarians. Each review describes and rates the book and also assesses the audience that it is most appropriate for. The ratings given by this site are particularly promising as a simple source of quantitative subject evaluation data. This data must be manually extracted by subscribers, however, and so this is not a simple source to use for large-scale evalutaions (Kousha and Thelwall, 2015b).

Public reviews on general book-based websites like Amazon.com and Goodreads provide an additional source of book reviews. These can be written by any user and some are posted anonymously by authors or by publishers and so they contain a degree of spam. Another limitation is that books on controversial topics may receive partisan reviews and books that attract much publicity may receive additional negative reviews as a result of reaching a wider audience. For example, prestigious book-prize winners can expect to start receiving a higher proportion of negative reviews as a result of their fame (Kovács and Sharkey, 2014). The reviews cover both academic and non-academic books and presumably are primarily written by people who have just read the book. Like Choice, these sites have ratings associated with reviews (on a five-point scale) and so can be used for their subjective evidence in addition to counting the number of reviews for each book. Data for books can be systematically extracted from Goodreads using its API and from Amazon with a combination of techniques (see Sections 8.15 and 8.16) and so both are practical sources of book review evidence for large-scale assessments. The ease with which they can be spammed rules them out from use in formal evaluations, however.

Coverage: Under a third of BkCI (Book Citation Index, in the Web of Science) monographs from 2008 had at least one Amazon review in the arts and humanities (31%), social science (25%), and science and medicine (29%) by mid 2014 (Kousha and Thelwall, 2016a). For a selection of 15,928 BkCI academic books in 2008–2010, most in the arts (85%), humanities (80%) and social sciences (67%) had at least one Goodreads review by 2015 (Kousha et al., in press).

Empirical evidence: Amazon review counts correlate with WoS/BkCI citations with low strengths, varying from 0.22 (social science) and 0.19 (arts and humanities) to 0.12 (science, engineering and medicine) (Kousha and Thelwall, 2016a). The number of reader ratings within

Goodreads has a low correlation of 0.21 with the number of citations to selected history books (Zuccala et al., 2015b). Ratings of books from the library-oriented magazine *Choice* have low positive correlations with Google Books citations (science and technology: 0.35; humanities: 0.14; social and behavioural sciences: 0.08) and with library holdings (science and technology: 0.27; humanities: 0.30; social and behavioural sciences: 0.12) (Kousha and Thelwall, 2015b). This evidence, having similarly low correlations with citation counts as sales and library holding data, suggests that reviews might reflect a different type of impact or, since they can be influenced by spam, may not reflect any type of impact.

Interpretation: Choice book ratings could be viewed as a usefulness indicator since the ratings are aimed at guiding librarians' purchasing strategies. It seems reasonable to also view them as proxy evidence of the likely readership of a book. Amazon and Goodreads review counts are usage indicators and average ratings can be used as popularity indicators.

3.9   BOOK SALES

Book sales are presumably a good indicator of audience size, although the figures ignore library lending and online reading. Since publisher sales are rarely available, sales ranks from online bookstores like Amazon.com may be used as a proxy. This assumes that online sales would be proportional to total sales but this is unlikely to be universally true.

Coverage: Presumably all academic books sell at least one copy, giving a coverage of 100%, but the key coverage issue is the proportion of books that register sales on public websites. Amazon.com does not report sales but reports sales ranks. These are dependent on both time and market rather than total sales, but seem to have a coverage of 100%.

Empirical evidence: Amazon.com sales ranks correlate with WoS/BkCI citations with low strengths, varying from 0.25 (arts and humanities) and 0.23 (social science) to 0.13 (science, engineering and medicine) (Kousha and Thelwall, 2016a). The low correlations suggest, but do not prove, that book purchases reflect non-scholarly impact to a substantial degree.

Interpretation: Sales ranks indicate book readership, with the precise nature of the value gained by the reading depending upon the type of book. This could include cultural, educational, scholarly or professional value. Thus the generic term usage indictor is appropriate.

3.10   LIBRARY HOLDINGS FOR BOOKS

The number of libraries holding a copy of a book seems to be a reasonable indicator of its likely readership (Torres-Salinas and Moed, 2009; White et al., 2009). It is imperfect because a popular novel might be continually checked out, with a long waiting list, and a course book might be in a university short loan collection so that a different person can check it out every day but other books might never be opened. Similarly, some books are marketed solely as reference works for libraries whereas others are primarily written for the general public.

It is possible to get systematic international evidence about the number of libraries holding a book from the WorldCat website by requesting a list of libraries holding a book from the book's ISBN or other key information (Figure 3.4). WorldCat is an organisation that seeks to maintain a comprehensive index of the books held by the world's libraries so that librarians and others can track down books for inter-library loans or direct borrowing. This combined catalogue information can be automatically gathered via an API, making library holdings a practical indicator for large collection of books. Permission must be first sought from WorldCat to use the API, which may delay its use in practice. Once an API key has been granted, Webometric Analyst can be used to extract the necessary information.

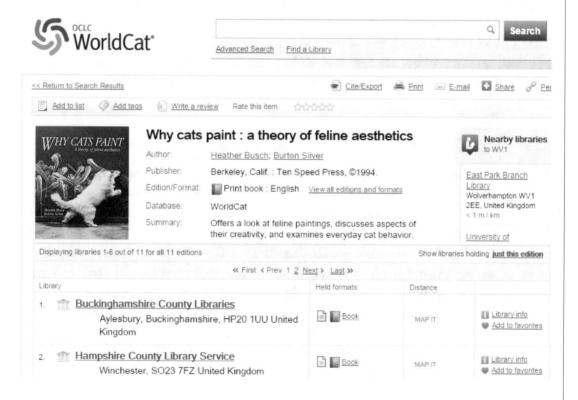

Figure 3.4: Library holdings for a book as reported by WorldCat.

Coverage: All of a sample of BkCI monographs from 2008 have at least one WorldCat library holding record in the arts and humanities, social science and science and medicine (Kousha and Thelwall, 2016a).

Empirical evidence: All BkCI monographs from 2008 are in at least one library. For these books, WorldCat library holdings correlate with WoS/BkCI citations with low strengths, varying from 0.15 (social science) and 0.14 (arts and humanities) to 0.09 (science, engineering and medicine) (Kousha and Thelwall, 2016a). An earlier study had found higher correlations in the humanities between WorldCat library holdings and Scopus citations for 2007–2011 books in history (0.28) and literature (0.25) (Zuccala and Guns, 2013). The difference may be due to the more extensive or more international coverage of Scopus. As with sales data, the low correlations suggest, but do not prove, that library holdings reflect a substantially different type of impact to traditional journal citation impact.

Interpretation: Despite the limitations discussed above it seems reasonable to use library holdings as evidence of the likely readership or usage of the book. This is a very general indicator description but a more specific phrase, such as scholarly, educational or cultural impact is inappropriate as a general term for all scholarly books because there are probably substantial numbers of academic books that have only one of these types of impacts. If the context of the reading is clear for a book or collection of books, then it would be reasonable to use a narrower term. For example, if the books were all literary novels, then library holdings could reasonably be called a cultural impact indicator.

3.11   ADVANCED WEB SERVER LOG FILE ANALYSIS

Web server log files record web requests for documents. These log files are routinely used by website owners to keep track of the usage of their site. They (or browser-based page tagging) are also used by publishers to count how often their articles are downloaded. Publishers and others given access to these log files can mine them for more detailed information to give a more fine-grained interpretation of the basic download counts. This extra detail can be deduced about many of the people requesting files. If they log on to a digital library, then their exact identity would be known and otherwise in most cases it is possible to infer their geographic location from their IP address. It is also possible to guess what type of person they are from their IP address to some extent. For example, a user accessing from a university IP address is likely to be a student or employee of the university. Similarly, someone accessing from a government or (some types of) commercial IP address is likely to be an employee of the organisation. Using this information, it is possible to construct audience-specific indicators for a digital library or repository.

Coverage: Permission is rarely given to access copies of web server log files so coverage is low in practical terms.

Empirical evidence: Visitors to an academic website can be automatically classified as to their likely broad user type (e.g., research, industry, government) with a high degree of accuracy (90%) from server log file information (Duin et al., 2012).

Interpretation: Advanced log file server accesses can give a set of audience-specific usage indicators. This is most simply accomplished by reporting the overall access count and the proportion from the main sources found from their IP addresses. Thus, given the ability to map IP addresses to sector types, web server log file analyses can give fine-grained impact evidence by splitting up the overall accesses into different types (e.g., educational, commercial, governmental).

3.12   SUMMARY

Usage, popularity and attention data are the most basic type of impact indicators since they do not point to any particular type of impact, although the type of impact may be clear from the context. Other factors being equal, it seems likely that documents and resources that have received more attention are likely to have had a bigger impact since being ignored is not a pathway to impact. Some of the indicators, such as library holdings, are numbers without any context and cannot therefore be checked for spam or investigated to get insights into usage contexts. In contrast, web citations, microblog and social network citations each have some associated text and so can be verified and examined in order to find out why they were created, giving the potential to check whether the results are meaningful and suggesting an impact type. Nevertheless, microblog citations seem too short to give a useful context in most cases. Usage indicators may be particularly helpful for individual non-standard resources (e.g., videos, software) to support a narrative claim for the type of impact that they have had.

CHAPTER 4

Academic, Commercial and Organisational Web Indicators

Some indicators are likely to reflect a specific type of impact rather than just usage. Several naturally express a type of academic impact. This applies to social bookmarking sites, because these are typically used by researchers, Google Books citations, because they are normally a type of academic citation, and blog citations, because scientific blog posts discussing research are often written by academics even if they target a wider audience. While one of the reasons for the drive to use alternative indicators to supplement citation counts has been to find evidence of non-academic impacts, new academic impact indicators can be employed to provide earlier evidence of impact (e.g., Mendeley, blog citations) or different aspects of academic impact (Google Books citations).

Patent citations have been used for many years as a commercial impact indicator because of the way that they connect knowledge to the right to profit from it. With the creation of the Google Patents service, patent citations can now be created from the web and this chapter covers web-derived patent indicators. Moreover, many businesses, governments and non-governmental organisations produce grey literature and so citations from online grey literature can be a source of organisational impact evidence.

4.1   MENDELEY AND SOCIAL BOOKMARKING/READER COUNTS

Mendeley is a free social reference recording and sharing website. Members can enter information about academic and other publications within the site and Mendeley will then help them to create reference lists for articles and will also save the information for possible future use. On the social side, members can browse the references of other users in order to find new papers (i.e., collaborative filtering). This might be useful because someone with a shared topic of interest or overlaps in their reference lists may have found other relevant papers. Members can connect with and communicate with each other, treating Mendeley as a virtual community or as a convenient site with which to communicate with their acquaintances. The large number of Mendeley users makes it a substantial source of evidence about interest in academic articles (Gunn, 2013).

Mendeley readership is currently the alternative indicator with the strongest empirical evidence to support its use, but has the disadvantage that it does not reflect a different type of impact to that of traditional citation counts. Mendeley readership counts are useful indicators of scholarly impact (see below), because they are numerically large (Costas et al., 2015a, 2015b) and occur sooner than do citations (Maflahi and Thelwall, 2016; Thelwall and Sud, in press). A researcher reading a paper can add it to their Mendeley library while conducting a study or writing it up, and this may well be at least a year earlier than the publication date of their paper. Thus, Mendeley can give earlier evidence of impact than can citations. This timeliness property is particularly helpful for research evaluations because these often need to examine recent publications.

Other social reference-sharing sites include Bibsonomy, CiteULike, Connotea and Zotero. These seem to have fewer users than Mendeley in most subject areas (e.g., Fenner, 2013; Li et al., 2012) and most lack an API to allow their data to be collected for research evaluation purposes. Bibsonomy reports the number of users that have registered an article on the site (called *bookmarking*), which is equivalent to the Mendeley reader count. Bibsonomy has an API (www.bibsonomy. org/help/doc/api.html) that does not report the number of users for an article and so is not useful for automating indicator data collection.

Coverage: For a set of journal articles and reviews 2010 and 2012 in both PubMed and WoS, the proportion with at least one Mendeley reader varied from 41% in the humanities to 81% in psychology (Haustein et al., 2014b; see also: Alhoori and Furuta, 2014; Zahedi et al., 2014a). Mendeley coverage may be similar for documents outside of the core WoS collection because 71% of Latin American journal articles from 2008 in one study had a Mendeley reader by 2014 (Alperin, 2015). For a selection of BkCI monographs from 2008, few in the arts and humanities (4%), social sciences (6%) and science and medicine (14%) had any Mendeley readers in mid-2014 (Kousha and Thelwall, 2016a). About 21% of recent articles from 785 high-impact science journals were bookmarked in CiteULike (Alhoori and Furuta, 2014).

Empirical evidence: Studies of many different academic fields have found Mendeley readership counts to have substantial positive correlations with citation counts. A first analysis showed that Mendeley reader counts correlated strongly with WoS citation counts for articles from the year 2007 in *Nature* (0.559, n=793) and *Science* (0.540, n=820) (Li et al., 2012). For broad disciplines, correlations with citations tend to be positive and moderate. Spearman correlations with WoS have been found for articles from 2008 for clinical medicine (0.463), engineering and technology (0.327), social science (0.456), physics (0.308) and chemistry (0.369) (Mohammadi et al., 2015), and in psychology (0.514), social sciences other subjects (0.403), education and education research (0.484), information science and library science (0.535), business and economics (0.573), philosophy (0.366), history (0.428), linguistics (0.454), literature (0.403) and religion (0.363) (Mohammadi and Thelwall, 2014). Within 45 more narrowly defined medical fields and relatively old articles from 2009, the correlation between Mendeley readers was even higher, averaging 0.7 (Thelwall and Wilson, 2016). One large-scale investigation compared Mendeley reader counts to peer review scores for articles submitted to the 2014 UK REF, finding substantial positive correlations in 32 out of 36 broad fields. The highest Spearman correlation was 0.441 (for clinical medicine, n=2070), using UK Research Excellence Framework 2014 data (HEFCE, 2015). The positive correlations tend to be low although a majority are at least 0.1; 8 of the 32 positive correlations above 0.2 and a further 10 between 0.1 and 0.2. Mendeley readership counts are internationally biased because its users are disproportionately likely to register articles written by people from their own country (Thelwall and Maflahi, 2015). The same is true for citations (Lancho-Barrantes et al., 2012) but the effect is probably more substantial in Mendeley than in traditional citation databases because the website seems to be far more popular in some countries than others (e.g., it was ranked 949 in Malaysia but only 10,693 in Japan in June 2016 according to Alexa: www.alexa.com/siteinfo/mendeley.com). There are moderate correlations between WoS citations and CiteULike bookmarks for articles in the journals *Science* and *Nature* (Li et al., 2012) and low positive correlations for papers in nine computer science conferences (Jiang et al., 2013). An analysis of Bibsonomy activity from 2006 to 2009 using a copy of its (private) web server logs found only a small positive correlation between bookmarks of articles in all disciplines and years and citation counts from Microsoft Academic Search (Zoller et al., 2016).

Interpretation: Although a paper does not have to be read before being registered in Mendeley, it seems reasonable to call the number of people that register a publication the Mendeley reader count. This can be justified by a survey of Mendeley users; most recorded articles that they had read or intended to read (Mohammadi et al., 2016). The high correlations found between Mendeley reader counts and Scopus citations discussed above, together with the few non-academic users suggest that the best interpretation is as a scholarly impact indicator. Nevertheless, its international bias in uptake and bias towards younger users (Mohammadi et al., 2015) mean that it should be accompanied by caveats. Thus, Mendeley reader counts are genuine scholarly readership indicators and also (early) scholarly impact indicators with a bias towards younger readers and international biases.

4.2   GOOGLE BOOKS CITATIONS

Google Books is a huge repository that seems to contain the vast majority of the world's books. It is the logical source of impact for book-based fields, and particularly for monographs. Google Books does not provide a citation index but it is possible to query it for book citations by entering the book title as a phrase search, adding the author name and publication year to narrow down the results. The results need to be filtered to identify correct matches since for some queries many results are not matches or are not citations. The query submission and results filtering can be automated with Webometric Analyst (Kousha and Thelwall, 2015a) and so citation counts from Google Books form a practical alternative indicator.

Coverage: Most BkCI monographs from 2008 had at least one Google Books citation in the arts and humanities (92%), social science (85%) and science and medicine (70%) by mid-2014

(Kousha and Thelwall, 2016a). For a selection of 15,928 BkCI academic books in 2008–2010, most in the arts and humanities (81–88%), social sciences (79–87%), science (53–70%), medicine (42–80%) and engineering (53–69%) had at least one Google Books citation by 2015 (Kousha et al., in press).

Empirical evidence: Google Books citations are about as frequent as WoS citations in the social sciences but only 4% as numerous in most sciences (exception: computing with 46% due to conference proceedings). In science, Spearman correlations with WoS citations are 0.15 to 0.35 (exception: Computing with 0.71); for social science they vary from 0.41 to 0.59 and in the humanities 0.36 to 0.65 (Kousha and Thelwall, 2009). In the humanities, Google books citations are 1.4–3.2 times as frequent as Scopus citations and the correlation between the two varies from 0.61 to 0.83 (Kousha et al., 2011). When compared with WoS citations incorporating the Book Citation Index (BkCI), the correlations tend to be higher. In the arts and humanities, the two sources give similar citation counts and correlations between 0.53 and 0.62. For the social sciences, Google Books has about two thirds as many citations as WoS/BkCI and correlations vary between 0.49 and 0.64. In medicine, science and engineering, there are a quarter as many Google Books citations as WoS/BkCI citations, with correlations between 0.24 and 0.50 (Kousha and Thelwall, 2015a). About a quarter of Malaysian university press books published 1961–2012 had been cited in Google Books compared to about a third with Google Scholar citations (Abdullah and Thelwall, 2014), so Google Books citations may be useful for non-Western nations. Overall, there is strong evidence of the value of Google Books citations for the social sciences, arts and humanities.

Interpretation: Book citation impact would be scholarly impact for the arts, humanities and social science fields that publish mainly in monographs or edited volumes. It can also be educational impact via citations in class textbooks for types of research in any field that are used in education. It could also be professional impact for types of research that are cited by professional education, information or training books. Although, as discussed above, citations from Google Books could reflect educational or professional impacts, it seems likely that most citations could reasonably be characterised as reflecting scholarly impact. Thus, unless the context of the books points clearly to an alternative type of impact, Google Books citations should be taken as scholarly impact indicators.

4.3   CITATIONS FROM BLOGS

Blogs are websites based around posts that are displayed in reverse chronological order—the latest first. Blogs were an early type of site that allowed casual users to post their thoughts to the web. Blogs are usually based within large blog hosting sites, such as blogger.com and Wordpress.com, with the site managing the content entered by the user in a relatively straightforward way. Although blogs are now more sophisticated in format and capabilities than early versions, they retain the focus of relatively informal posts of a few paragraphs of text, with or without associated images or videos, about issues of interest to the owner.

Blogs are different from microblogs because they have room for a full description or evaluation of academic articles and because their format does not lend them to general publicity use. The reason is that there is no equivalent of the news feed that has anything approaching the reach of microblog sites like Twitter and Sina Weibo.

Of particular interest are science blogs because these focus on academic research. Some exclusively review academic articles, others discuss specific issues, such as ethics or a given research field, or cover a more ad-hoc range of topics. Blogs were historically designed to publish text to the world rather than specific friends or followers, and the substantial nature of blog posts compared to microblog posts gives the promise that citations from blogs, or from science blogs, will give stronger impact evidence than would microblog posts. Nevertheless, far fewer people keep blogs and so blog posts about science are likely to be much rarer than microblog posts about science, which undermines the value of blog-based indicators. In addition, blog posts are awkward to systematically harvest for citations because they originate from many different blog hosting sites and they have complex formats that make it difficult to automatically extract citations.

Science aggregators can help to identify relevant blogs and blog posts, because they are services that list blog posts about public academic research. Articles registered in ResearchBlogging.org, for example, must obey minimum quality standards and cite research in a standard format (Shema et al., 2014). Nevertheless, blog posts citing academic research are currently difficult to harvest on a large scale.

Coverage: About 17% of recent articles from 785 high-impact science journals had been blogged at least once according to altmetric.com data (Alhoori and Furuta, 2014). This figure seems to be unrealistically high, perhaps including publicity blogs as well as science blogs.

Empirical evidence: Research articles that are the subject of science blog postings are likely to attract more citations in the future than comparable articles (Shema et al., 2014), although it is not clear if the correlation occurs because blog post publicity generates future citations. Science blog citations are nevertheless valid as early evidence of likely future citation impact. If the higher future citation impact of blogged articles is entirely due to the blog post publicity, then this would undermine blog citations as a research quality indicator but does not necessarily undermine their value as an academic impact indicator. The value of blog citations is corroborated by science blog posts tending to be in-depth critical reviews, at least in the health domain (Shema et al., 2015).

Interpretation: Science blog posts can be treated as high quality interest evidence because they seem to be predominantly carefully constructed, especially if they are indexed in a science blog aggregator (Shema et al., 2015). They may also be valid indicators of academic impact for collections of articles, but more evidence is needed to confirm this and to investigate whether blog posts generate future citations to the articles discussed.

4.4   CITATIONS FROM PATENTS

Patents are official documents that describe inventions and, when granted, allow the inventors to legally defend the right to use the invention within a specified country or countries. Especially in the U.S., patents sometimes include citations to other patents and citations to other documents (sometimes called non-patent citations). These citations can reference any type of document, including journal articles, books and videos. Since the purpose of a patent is to defend the right to sell an invention, it seems intuitively possible that a citation reflects technology transfer or the commercial relevance for the cited documents. Bing can be used to identify patent citations through the Google Patents website with queries, including information such as the first author last name, the article title in quotes, the publication year and site to restrict the results to the patent site (Kousha and Thelwall, in press-b), as follows:

```
Vidic "Uptake of elemental mercury vapors by activated
carbons" 1996 site:google.com/patents
```

Coverage: For Scopus articles in 1996–2012 in applied science and engineering fields, coverage varied from 2% (mechanical engineering) to 10% (biomedical engineering) (Kousha and Thelwall, in press-b). Coverage is likely to be much lower outside of these areas and close to 0% in the arts, humanities and social sciences.

Empirical evidence: Counts of citations from patents have a weak (0.05 to 0.36) positive correlation with Scopus citation counts in applied science and engineering fields (Kousha and Thelwall, in press-b; Tijssen et al., 2000). The most important drawback of their use is that they are rare. Probably less than 1% of articles in Scopus have been cited by U.S. patents and the highest percentage is up to 10% for some biomedical engineering specialisms (Kousha and Thelwall, in press-b).

Interpretation: Patent citation counts can be claimed to represent usefulness or relevance to commercial innovation. This is not universally true, however, because the cited articles may often have not directly motivated the invention described in the patent. A minority may have been added by patent examiners rather than the inventor (Tijssen et al., 2000) and therefore probably have not helped the invention (Jaffe et al., 2000). Inventor citations may use standard works (e.g., textbooks) to help describe well-known non-novel aspects of the invention. Citations in patents are therefore not strong evidence of technology transfer (Meyer, 2000). Thus, commercial relevance seems to be a better general term for patent indicators than technology transfer.

4.5   CITATIONS FROM THE GREY LITERATURE? PDF AND DOC FILES

A simple way to gather citations from web documents that are likely to reflect a substantial amount of impact is to narrow down the document type of the citing documents to common report formats (Wilkinson et al., 2014). Although many papers are posted online in standard web (HTML) format, important reports often have PDF format as their primary form because this forms a record of the printed version. Other reports are sometimes posted online in the file format of the software used to produce them, such as Microsoft Word. It is therefore possible that searching the web for citations, but narrowing down the results to just PDF and Word documents would ensure that most of the matches were informally produced documents, such as the grey literature. Grey literature citations are tracked by Altmetric.com, for example. Of course, many journal articles and conference papers are also posted online in PDF and Word formats and so the results may also include a mix of these. Other document types that may be found online in a special format include Ph.D. theses, student projects, free magazines and newsletters.

Web citations in a given file format can be searched for in Google and Bing with the use of the advanced search command filetype: followed by the appropriate file name extension. This restricts the results to a given document or file format. To get PDF matches only, the command filetype:pdf should be added to the end of the query as follows:

```
"Shit happens The selling of risk in extreme sport"
Palmer 2002 "Australian Journal of Anthropology" file-
type:pdf
```

To get Word format document matches only, the command filetype:doc should be added to the end of the query instead. There is no need to also use other Microsoft Word file name extensions, such as docx and rtf, because they are included in the results for doc.

```
"Reusing treated effluent in concrete technology" Lee
2001 "Jurnal teknologi" filetype:doc
```

Coverage: The proportion of documents cited in the grey literature depends on the set analysed. This can be expected to be high for sets of key documents produced by important organisations but low for more routine documents or those produced by unknown groups.

Empirical evidence: There is no empirical evidence for this alternative indicator yet.

Interpretation: The most reasonable interpretation of web PDF or Word citation counts depends on the genre and purpose of the cited documents investigated. If the cited documents are academic journal articles, then the citation counts are likely to be dominated by online copies of other journal articles (including the publisher and author versions of the articles), and so the counts would form a predominantly academic impact indicator. In some areas, citing student dissertations and online course syllabi might also be common, so the indicator would then reflect both academic and educational impacts. In contrast, if the cited documents examined predominantly target a non-academic audience (e.g., governments, business users) and it is clear that this is the nature of most web citations (e.g., government white papers, business newsletters) then it would be reasonable to interpret the counts as reflecting government or business interest, respectively.

4.6   BOOK PUBLISHER PRESTIGE

With only partial exceptions (SENSE, 2009), academic book publisher prestige rankings are not currently available online, but these are mentioned here briefly as a likely future web indicator. In the arts and humanities, publishers have different levels of selectivity about the books that they publish, and getting a volume published by a prestigious publisher is an important marker that a book is likely to be important. A good publisher would presumably also help a book to reach a wide audience. Book publisher information is public and this is therefore another possible book-specific indicator, although not a web indicator. Some national research assessment exercises use teams of experts to categorise publishers into different prestige bands in order to help book assessments (Verleysen and Engels, 2013). Prestige is an informal concept but can be operationalised by the field and year normalised average number of citations per book (Torres-Salinas et al., 2012; Zuccala et al., 2015a). Studies that have asked scholars to rank publishers have obtained similar answers in most cases, at least at the top of the ranking list (Garand and Giles, 2011; Giménez-Toledo et al., 2013; Metz and Stemmer, 1996), although there are national and disciplinary differences in perceptions.

4.7   SUMMARY

In contrast to citations from the Web of Science or Scopus, the academic web indicators discussed here offer earlier evidence (Mendeley readers, science blogs), or evidence of a different type of academic impact (Google Books). Both Mendeley reader data and Google Books citations can be gathered automatically for large samples of documents, and so these are practical sources of academic impact evidence. Patent indicators can also be gathered automatically and give evidence of potential commercial impact, but their utility is restricted to areas of science in which patenting is common. While organisational impact indicators can also be automatically gathered on a large scale, there is no concrete evidence of their worth. Nevertheless, it seems likely that they would give helpful evidence for people and organisations that produce grey literature that does not target an academic audience but is intended to be read by government, industry or the public.

CHAPTER 5

Educational Impact Indicators

An important part of the role of universities, and many academics, is higher education. In support of this, lecturers may write textbooks for students, and social sciences and humanities scholars may write monographs that at least partly target undergraduate or postgraduate students. Although there are disciplinary differences in educational approaches (Neumann, 2001), research articles are sometimes used in the classrooms even in science, giving them extra value in addition to their primary scholarly communication role. Indicators of educational impact can therefore be used to assess academic contributions to teaching and learning. Although the potential educational value of publications seems to be rarely acknowledged in research revaluations, this is an omission because supporting higher education is clearly a useful scholarly outcome and public good.

Within this chapter, syllabus mentions give the clearest evidence of educational impact, whereas both PowerPoint and Wikipedia citations combine educational and other types of impacts. In some contexts, the usage indicators above can also provide educational impact (e.g., library holdings for course textbooks).

5.1 SYLLABUS MENTIONS

The most straightforward way to assess the use of scholarly outputs in higher education is to count how often they are used in courses. The logical source of information about this is the course syllabus because it normally lists essential and recommended readings for students. While such recommendations are unreliable because some may be perfunctory and others may be out of date, they are at least an official and reasonably standardised source of class reading information. Although there isn't a universal standardised register of higher education syllabi, some are posted to the public web and could, in theory, be scanned for reading lists. A limitation of this is that an unknown proportion of the world's syllabi is public. While there is an increasing trend to post syllabi online, they are probably in password-protected virtual learning environments or intranets in most cases. Nevertheless, it is possible to find syllabi that cite a particular work by Googling the title of the work (adding the author last name, year and publication to narrow down the query), then adding the term *syllabus* or *course description*, as follows.

```
Ryan "Kissing brides and loving hot vampires" "Sex
Education" 2016 syllabus
```

```
Ryan "Kissing brides and loving hot vampires" "Sex
Education" 2016 "course description"
```

While such a search may generate many false matches, it is possible to filter out those that are not from university websites manually for individual cases or automatically using Webometric Analyst's pre-set university list in order to get a more reliable figure. This is likely to be a substantial underestimate of the use of the resource in higher education due to the absence of private online syllabi from the results but it is also concrete evidence of educational impact.

Coverage: The prevalence of syllabus citations varies greatly by discipline and document type. An early study estimated that the average number of syllabus citations per Web of Science article ranged from minute (0.0008: analytical chemistry) to moderate (0.51: business) (Kousha and Thelwall, 2008). For Scopus-indexed books in 2005–2010, between 23% (physics and astronomy) and 56% (arts and humanities) have at least one syllabus citation (Kousha and Thelwall, in press-a).

Empirical evidence: The first study also found a low statistically significant positive Spearman correlation of 0.231 between citation counts and syllabus mentions within the single field analysed in detail: information science and library science (Kousha and Thelwall, 2008). An investigation of syllabus mentions of academic books found positive and significant Spearman correlations with Scopus citations in all subjects examined. The coefficients varied from 0.110 (chemistry) to 0.522 (social sciences), confirming the value of syllabus citations in the social sciences (Kousha and Thelwall, in press-a). Syllabus mentions have also been shown to correlate positively with the number of awards and grants received by a small group of social sciences and humanities scholars in Taiwan (Chen et al., 2015).

Interpretation: Syllabus mentions reflect (higher) educational impact because a syllabus citation is advice to students about what to read to help them to understand their course. Although syllabi can be created outside of universities for professional training and for teaching children, these are not likely to frequently cite academic research. Non-academic syllabi are also excluded by automatic methods to gather syllabus mentions.

5.2   CITATIONS IN POWERPOINT FILES

Academics give presentations at conferences and lectures to students. Sometimes these are supported by PowerPoint slides, sometimes these slides are supported by references and sometimes these slides are subsequently placed online. Assuming that non-academic presenters rarely put their slides on the public web or do not include formal citations to academic research in them, PowerPoint citations should tend to reflect either academic or educational impacts of research. It is possible to find online PowerPoint files citing research using commercial search engines because they index the content of PowerPoint slides. PowerPoint-specific queries can be built by appending the advanced search command filetype:ppt to the end of information about the publication (this includes pptx files).

```
Bourke "Dismembering the Male: Men's Bodies, Britain,
and the Great War" 1996 filetype:ppt
```

There are many limitations with using PowerPoint citation counts as an impact indicator. Most presentations are probably not posted to the public web, with many posted instead to private virtual learning environments. Some disciplines may rarely bother with presentation slides but may talk instead, or may support their talks with other presentation formats, such as PDF. Many lecturers do not share their slides with students or with conference attendees, particularly if the latter can access proceedings summarising their talk or giving a full paper that the talk was based on. International differences in the extent to which academics post resources online are also likely to bias the citation counts. Even though sites like SlideShare make it possible for all web users to share slides online without charge it is likely that this is done more systematically in richer nations than in others.

Coverage: A small minority of academic articles have PowerPoint citations, with disciplinary differences (Thelwall and Kousha, 2008; Kousha et al., 2010a).

Empirical evidence: There is no correlation-based evidence of the value of PowerPoint citations.

Interpretation: Counting citations from online presentations can usually be expected to give indicators for a combination of academic and educational impact (Thelwall and Kousha, 2008). The exact combination of the two probably varies by discipline and it is possible that in some fields professional presentations with citations are numerous enough to change the type of impact that PowerPoint citations reflect.

5.3   CITATIONS IN WIKIPEDIA

Wikipedia is one of the most popular international websites and serves as a repository of knowledge that is drawn upon by school pupils and university students for their education, professionals to aid their jobs and individual citizens for recreational activities. Although, like academic publications, it contains knowledge, it is not restricted to scholarly knowledge. Nevertheless, its articles frequently draw upon academic references to support its entries and therefore can potentially mediate between scholarship and the wider public in the transmission of information in an understandable format. Because of this, citations from Wikipedia entries may give evidence about the usefulness of academic outputs for topics of interest to the public and education (Nielsen, 2007; Kousha and Thelwall, in press-c).

Citations from Wikipedia can be identified by Bing searches restricted to the Wikipedia website and mentioning the first author last name, the first few terms of the article title and publication year, as follows. Articles with short titles can include the journal name as an additional phrase search. A practical limitation is that some articles are copied from one language version of Wikipedia to another, generating multiple citations from a single source and arguably exaggerating the value of the cited article (Kousha and Thelwall, in press-c).

```
Schmidtberger "Wax On, Wax Off: Pubic Hair Grooming
and Potential Complications" 2014 site:wikipedia.org/
wiki
```

Coverage: About 5% of academic articles seems to be cited in Wikipedia (Kousha and Thelwall, in press-c). Just over a third of a selection of 15,928 BkCI academic books in 2008–2010 had at least one Wikipedia citation by 2015 in the arts (58–61%), humanities (48–54%), social sciences (30–39%), medical sciences (18–34%), science (23–35%) and engineering (18–37%) (Kousha et al., in press).

Empirical evidence: Wikipedia and Scopus citations correlate at a low level of about 0.1 for articles, depending on the field analysed, and a moderate level of about 0.3 for monographs, again depending on the field analysed (Kousha and Thelwall, in press-c). Wikipedia citations may have a bias towards prestigious journals (Nielsen, 2007).

Interpretation: Wikipedia citations probably tend to reflect educational or general informational impact, depending on the subject area and topic of the cited document (Kousha and Thelwall, in press-c).

5.4   SUMMARY

The three educational impact indicators discussed here, Wikipedia citations, PowerPoint citations and syllabus mentions, can all be gathered automatically and so are practical sources of evidence about the educational impacts of research. Both Wikipedia citations and PowerPoint citations may also partly reflect non-educational research impacts and so these must be used cautiously as educational impact indicators. All three are relatively rare and therefore would be most useful to compare large sets of documents. For this application, averages or other relevant indicator formulae could be calculated for each set of documents and then compared between sets. The indicators could also be employed as evidence to support a specific claim that a small set of documents was having a particularly strong impact in education.

CHAPTER 6

Medical Impact Indicators

Medical and health-related research is in a special position within academia. Not only can research findings directly affect the health of individual humans but also the way in which research influences the decisions of professionals increasingly needs to be transparent and publicly regulated. In addition, individual medical studies frequently seem to be very expensive and subjected to a great degree of post-publication scrutiny. As a result of the apparent high value of medical research, this is the only area in which there is a large post-publication peer review website, F1000, and the only area in which there is a systematic provision of research-informed professional guidelines. These two have created opportunities for unique medical impact indicators, although all are awkward to collect on a large scale for impact evaluations. In principle, these indicators can be calculated for publications from all fields of research but, in practice, they are likely only to be relevant to health-related disciplines.

6.1 F1000PRIME RECOMMENDATIONS

The Faculty of 1000 website F1000Prime contains reviews and ratings (1, 2 or 3 stars, corresponding to Good, Very Good and Exceptional) of published biomedical research. It is a subscription-based service that offers subscribers judgements about current research. The site's reviewers are paid experts from a wide range of relevant fields. Although articles that have gone through peer review should be correct and relatively problem-free, especially if published in a reputable medical journal, these reviews also include judgements about the type of audience that may find them useful and the type of value that they might provide. Thus, the site can be used for evidence of non-academic impacts. F1000 also ranks articles based upon the total number of stars awarded from all reviews, although it previously used to rank articles with a more complex formula with a similar overall effect. Since F1000 data is not public and has no API, its values need to be paid for and manually collected by subscribers unless F1000 would be willing to provide a copy of its database for indicator applications (e.g., Waltman and Costas, 2014).

Coverage: About 23% of recent articles from 785 high impact science journals were registered in F1000 (Alhoori and Furuta, 2014). These were presumably all relevant to biomedical science.

Empirical evidence: Low to moderate correlations have been found between F1000 scores and citation counts. An investigation of F1000 scores for 49 Wellcome Trust-funded papers found a significant positive correlation (0.445) with expert reviewer judgements, suggesting that F1000 scores are broadly reasonable (Allen et al., 2009). For 1,397 Genomics and Genetics articles from

2008 and rated in F1000, their WoS citations correlated significantly (0.3) with their F1000 scores (Li and Thelwall, 2012). A Spearman correlation of 0.4 has also been found between WoS citations and F1000 scores for 125 articles from 2008 in WoS and F1000 (Bornmann and Leydesdorff, 2013). An analysis of 38,327 F1000-rated standard articles and reviews from 2006–09 within WoS (almost all publications matching these criteria) used a two-year citation and rating window. Within WoS subject categories, the highest proportion of articles that were rated by F1000 was 12% in Multidisciplinary Sciences. This study found a correlation of 0.24 between the highest rating given to an article and its citation count (Waltman and Costas, 2014). F1000 ratings associate more strongly with the impact factors of the publishing journal than the citation counts of articles (Eyre-Walker and Stoletzki, 2013) with the latter being a marginally better indicator of article quality. F1000 labels have also been researched. An investigation of F1000 labels found that two out of seven associated with citation counts. Articles tagged "New finding" or "Changes clinical practice" tended to be more cited than other articles, with the latter being a particularly strong indicator since it implies direct health impacts on society (Mohammadi and Thelwall, 2013).

Interpretation: Although there is no direct empirical evidence to support this specific claim, the F1000Prime "changes clinical practice" tag is an indicator of likely societal health benefits since at least one F1000 referee believed that professional practice would change as a result of the research. The highest star rating awarded to an article is a peer review quality judgement, and the total number of stars awarded is hybrid quality and interest evidence. Either academic impact or medical impact would be appropriate terms for these.

6.2   CITATIONS IN CLINICAL GUIDELINES

Early medical practitioners made their own rules for treatments, perhaps guided by their training, custom and practice in their field, medical books, previous experience and their intuition. Today, official documents provide recommendations about what to do in particular cases. No health practitioner can be an expert on all of the conditions that they face and so standardised advice from panels of experts can help in new situations. The UK's main advice for health professionals is contained in the NICE (National Institute for Health and Care Excellence) Guidelines that are produced by panels of experts for each topic and are supported by an extensive collection of academic references. A citation from this source would therefore be good evidence that research is informing clinical practice.

An important limitation of clinical guideline citations is that although the guidelines themselves should be carefully and systematically constructed, the same is not necessarily true for their associated references. In particular, the references seem likely to contain relevant work from expert panel members more assiduously than other documents. They also contain non-primary research, such as systematic reviews and meta-analyses. Hence, the lack of a clinical guideline citation does not signify absence of influence if a paper is cited in another document that is itself cited. There are also likely to be national biases in guideline citations and few countries seem to publish guidelines and associated citations online and so a document may not be cited in a public guideline if it is influential in countries that don't produce or publish them. A practical limitation is that there is no citation index for guideline citations and so they need to be identified through web searches or systematically extracted from public guideline documents through specialist software.

Coverage: Probably less than 1% of all articles from any field are cited in clinical guidelines.

Empirical evidence: Articles cited in the clinical knowledge summaries underlying the U.K. NICE practitioner guidelines tend to be substantially more highly cited than comparable articles, although this is not evident for articles that are less than three years old (Grant et al., 2000; Thelwall and Maflahi, 2016).

Interpretation: Guideline citations are medical impact indicators. More specifically, they are indicators of societal health impact. While not all guideline citations directly improve societal health, the presence of a guideline citation is an indicator that this is possible.

6.3   CITATIONS IN CLINICAL TRIALS

Important basic medical research may not be recognised by clinical trial citations or F1000 recommendations because of the time delay between the publication of an innovative idea and its translation into health practice. One way of identifying medical research that promises future health benefits is to trace citations in clinical trials documents because clinical trials can be important intermediary steps between an initial idea and its government approval. Identifying references in clinical trials records has become possible through websites like ClinicalTrials.gov that contain a public record of clinical trials from over 190 countries, sometimes with supporting references. In the U.S., all clinical trials must be publicly registered in the ClinicalTrials.gov website, and so it is a systematic record of trials in this country and it also contains some trial documentation from other countries.

Coverage: Probably less than 1% of all articles from any field are cited in clinical trials.

Empirical evidence: Articles in four general medical journals tend to have more Scopus citations if they have been cited in the U.S. site ClinicalTrials.gov (Thelwall and Kousha, in press-b), and so clinical trials citations reflect citation impact to some extent.

Interpretation: Clinical trials citations are medical impact indicators of the potential health benefits of research. Since few clinical trials result in approved new medications (Contopoulos-Ioannidis et al., 2003), although others may support new practices rather than medications, these citations are not *predictors* of future health benefits. A citation from a clinical trial record can still be viewed as an indicator that an article is more *likely* to have an eventual health benefit than uncited articles.

6.4   SUMMARY

The three medical impact indicators all give evidence of medical or health impacts, with clinical guideline citations giving the most direct evidence. Clinical guideline citations are also relatively immune from deliberate manipulation since they are public and compiled by subject experts. Their biggest disadvantage is their relative scarcity. F1000Prime recommendations are also the results of expert judgements and are probably more common than guideline citations and thus are an attractive source of medical impact evidence, although they are not free and can't be automatically harvested for large sets of documents. Clinical trials citations offer the lowest quality evidence because they can be manipulated. They are also relatively rare but offer the promise of early impact evidence, which is their main advantage. All of these indicators are not straightforward to collect, although it is possible to gather clinical trials citations and clinical guideline citations with the aid of a web crawler.

CHAPTER 7

Applications

This chapter provides recommendations about how to use web indicators for literature searching, library management and academic self-promotion, as well as for evaluations by departments, institutions, non-academic organisations, funding agencies and countries. There are two important dimensions of difference between these applications. First, they can be evaluative with stakeholder interest in the results, or formative to aid internal decision making or reflection. For evaluations, the use of web indicators is only acceptable if the possibility of stakeholder manipulation of the data is minimal. Second, evaluations can focus on the individual web indicator values of small sets of outputs or could compare the aggregate impact of larger sets of outputs in order to evaluate the overall level of impact.

7.1   PUBLISHERS AND LITERATURE SEARCHERS

Publishers' websites increasingly incorporate web and citation indicators for individual articles as a metadata service for literature searchers and authors. One of the most systematic approaches for an individual publisher is the basket of "article level metrics" shown for each individual PLOS article (Figure 7.1) (Lin and Fenner, 2013; Neylon and Wu, 2009). This includes citation, usage and social media indicators. The inclusion of the number of times that each article has been cited in Scopus or WoS can help literature searches by helping to identify articles that are more important to academics, other factors being equal. This is also the reason why academic literature search interfaces, such as that of Google Scholar, incorporate citation counts within their keyword search results ranking algorithms and display them on results pages.

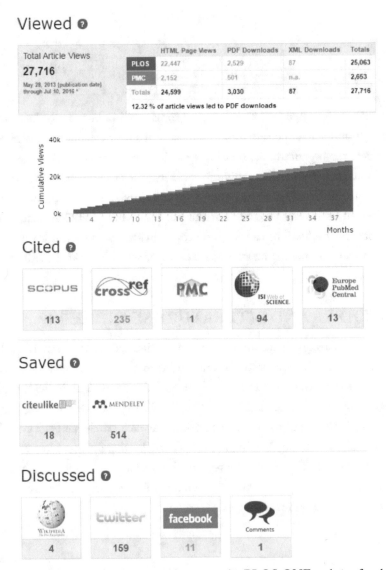

Figure 7.1: Some PLOS article-level metrics shown on the PLOS ONE website for the article "Do Altmetrics Work."

The citation counts for recently published literature are mainly zero and so are of little use for people conducing current awareness searching or browsing to identify important new literature. This gap is being filled by web indicators because they tend to occur much earlier than do citations (Adie and Roe, 2013; Holmberg, 2015). As a practical issue, indicators from social websites with an API (i.e., altmetrics) are particularly useful because they are easy to keep up-to-date, which is important for this role. This information can be gathered by publishers directly from social websites via APIs or indirectly from an altmetric data provider that will take care of the programming and data matching issues. The advantage of using an altmetric data provider is that they can gather data types, such as blog citations, that may be too time consuming to be practical for individual publishers to gather for themselves. In the future, the collection of social web indicators for journal articles may be helped by the provision of a unifying Crossref architecture, which was under development in 2016 (eventdata.crossref.org).

Within publisher websites, web indicators tend to serve as attention indicators for literature searchers rather than indicators of specific types of impact (e.g., educational, commercial) due the absence of social web indicators for more specific impact types. Because of this, the difference between the indicators is not important and the basket of metrics approach is pragmatic: showing all the indicators for which each article has a positive score (Figures 7.1, 7.2). Nevertheless, web indicators of specific types of impacts would be useful to help readers to identify articles with a specific type of value (e.g., commercial, educational) and to inform authors about the audience for their article. This has been recognised by Altmetric.com, which includes English Wikipedia citations and public policy document citations within its set of indicators (www.altmetric.com/about-our-data/our-sources/). These indicators are more complex to collect due to the lack of an API and therefore may only be practical for publishers to obtain from alternative indicator data providers.

Figure 7.2: The mini Altmetric.com donut on the home page of an article in the Wiley Online Library in July 2016, showing the brief additional indicator details revealed when the mouse hovers on the badge. Clicking on the "See more details" link reveals additional geographic and demographic information about the indicator sources.

Web indicators can also be useful for the authors of an article to give them early evidence about how much attention their article has attracted. This may help them to decide whether the line or research represented by the article is likely to be fruitful in terms of being recognised as interesting by others. Raw indicator scores need benchmarking in order to interpret whether they are high or low in comparison to similar articles, however. This can be achieved by reporting the percentile that the article falls in within its publication year and field, or the same field and journal. This approach is taken by Altmetric.com (Figure 7.3). PLOS instead only reports benchmarking information for its views indicator and it does this by reporting (graphically) the average number of views over time for articles from the same subject and year.

Figure 7.3: An Altmetric.com donut in the Wiley Online Library, showing benchmarking information underneath.

In summary, publishers are providing web indicators for articles on their websites to authors and literature searchers. These indicators can be gathered directly using APIs or indirectly via altmetric data providers. They are primarily from the social web and serve as attention indicators, but web indicators of specific types of impacts have been recently introduced and are a promising new development. In the future it is likely that some authors will spam web indicators in order to give their articles the impression of having attracted attention, and this may undermine the value of the indicators if it becomes prevalent and cannot be combatted.

7.2   INDIVIDUAL AUTHORS

Academics are increasingly required to justify their research time by demonstrating the value of their work. This may occur in the form of a grant, appointment, award or promotion application, a periodic national research assessment exercise or an informal progress review. Individual scholars may also wish to monitor their own progress or evaluate the impact of their outputs in order to plan their future work. Demonstrating or assessing value can be difficult because the societal or scholarly benefits of academic research are often evident only in the long term. In the short term, scholars may report their tangible outputs, such as articles or books, but not all of these outputs are equally valuable. Researchers may therefore need to make a case for the quality, value or impact of their outputs. Other than calling upon the judgements of peers, perhaps the most long-established justification is to point to the prestige of the publication outlet, such as the academic journal, book publisher or exhibition-hosting art gallery. A simple alternative for journal articles is to refer to the Journal Impact Factor (JIF—see Section 7.8) as an indicator of journal prestige. This has the advantage of being a relatively transparent number easily available for all fields. The JIF is often given too much importance because it is affected by spurious factors, however, such as the speed at which articles in a journal attract citations (Seglen, 1998). It should also not be compared between fields.

The most common direct impact indicator for academic articles, papers and books is the citation count: the number of times that they have has been cited by documents indexed in a major database, such as the Web of Science (WoS), Scopus or Google Scholar. Citation counts can be reported by academics as scholarly impact indicators for individual publications. The many ways in which new knowledge can be valuable without generating any citations, such as by generating industrial applications or informing practitioners, and web indicators can give evidence of these. In addition, web indicators can be used for evidence of the impact of many non-standard outputs, such as databases, software and videos. No academic can expect their research to have an impact in all possible ways and so individual researchers should find indicators that reflect the type of impact that their research has had, ignoring the remainder. In concrete terms, academics knowing that their research has primarily scholarly impact should look for citation indicators (book-based citation indicators in the arts and humanities); those having educational impact should investigate education-oriented alternative indicators (e.g., syllabus mentions, PowerPoint citations); those having applied impact should investigate patent citations; and those having wider societal impact should investigate attention, usage, sales or review indicators. These values should be benchmarked, if possible, such as with a claim that they are in the top X% for a field and year.

This approach can be followed by annotating CVs with supporting indicator data, by maintaining evidence-based cover letters or by maintaining a short portfolio of evidence of skills, achievements and impacts (e.g., ACUMEN Portfolio, 2014). If there are many outputs, then it is worth highlighting the evidence for selected key outputs rather than to exhaustively provide evidence for each one. Some narrative context and benchmarking figures (e.g., top X%) would help to clarify each impact claim. The use of a narrative also allows attention and usage indicators to be claimed to reflect more specific types of impact, if the type of impact is clear from the context.

Like CVs, cover letters can be a useful device for researchers to use to explain their research contribution, whether for job applications, funding applications, promotions, annual monitoring or self-evaluations. Researchers can create and periodically update cover letters to describe their core contributions to research, supporting these claims with indicator evidence. This document can then be used, with some tailoring, for situations when the researcher needs to make the case for the value of their work. It can either be updated each time it is used, each time important research progress is made, or periodically for self-evaluation purposes. Probably many people keep their cover letters from one job application to another and so this proposal just formalises that procedure. Maintaining such a letter has the advantage that it would be readily available and could be easily used in situations in which it is not specifically called for, such as annual progress reviews.

In summary, web indicators can help academics to self-assess or demonstrate early impact for their outputs as well as to help them make the case for their work having specific types of impact. Unless particularly large numbers of outputs are involved, relevant web indicator data can be obtained for individual outputs from publisher websites, altmetric data provider sites (e.g., Impact-Story, Altmetric.com) or with the manual techniques described in the preceding chapters. For large sets of publications, indicators could be collected only for the most important outputs.

7.3   ASSESSING ACADEMIC DEPARTMENTS AND RESEARCH GROUPS: INDIVIDUAL OUTPUTS

Academic departments and research groups sometimes need to provide their institution or other funding bodies with evidence of the value of their knowledge creation, such as through the UK REF and other national research assessment processes. They may also periodically self-assess their progress and look for areas of strength and weakness to support their internal decision making. Although value can be created in many ways, such as through business or community engagement, it can be evaluated in part by assessing the value of each of their outputs individually. In this case the most accurate and robust evaluation method is to use peer review. This peer review can be systematically aided by citation indicators (e.g., either field-normalised citation counts or citation counts reported alongside the field and year average) to cross check human judgements, to resolve differences between judges or to point to high or low quality outputs to examine particularly carefully (as in the UK REF2014). In other cases, the purpose of an evaluation (e.g., formative self-evaluations) may not justify the expense of peer review and so indicators could then completely replace some (e.g., in the Italian VQR national assessment: Abramo and D'Angelo, 2015) or all peer review, accepting the likely lower quality of the results.

Web indicators can be used to help evaluate individual academic departments or research groups for formal evaluations, if the researchers cannot manipulate them in advance, and also for self-evaluations. Web indicators can be used for formal evaluations of research groups if the groups are not told in advance about the indicators that will be used (i.e., surprise evaluations). Advance knowledge of the indicators would provide the assessed group with an unfair and counterproductive incentive to manipulate them. When transparency and advance agreement of assessment methods are important, this rules out web indicators (Wouters and Costas, 2012). When no advance warning of assessment methods is given it is reasonable in principle to provide web indicators as long as they are accompanied by appropriate explanations, warnings and caveats so that they are not given an unjustified weighting by the human assessors that interpret them.

The choice of web indicator can either be driven by the basket approach—collecting all available data—or by the type of societal impacts claimed by the assessed group (e.g., educational, commercial, organisational, societal), by the need for timeliness, or by the types outputs assessed if these are not restricted to traditional academic publications. These indicators can either aid peer review judgements about the individual assessed outputs or be used to identify individual outputs that have had important impacts. In the former case, background information about the reliability of the web indicators and their main types of bias should be provided to the reviewers. As with citations, the purpose of the web indicators in this context is to help the experts to make their judgements by providing an initial estimate, an arbitrator for difficult cases, or an independent source of evidence to cross-check their initial conclusions. Whichever approach is taken, assessors should be aware that individual outputs may have high values by chance.

Indicators that point to different types of impact can also be used to inform the design of a research evaluation by helping to identify the strengths and weaknesses of the groups in advance of a peer assessment (Moed and Halevi, 2015).

In summary, web indicators can support formal evaluations when those assessed do not know the indicator choice in advance, give information about a group to guide the design of its peer evaluation or help a department or research group's self-evaluation.

7.4   ACADEMIC DEPARTMENTS AND RESEARCH GROUPS: SETS OF PUBLICATIONS

The outputs of departments or research groups are sometimes collectively evaluated for national research assessments that compare all similar departments within a country. For this, an impact indicator formula needs to be selected in addition to indicators to reflect the types of impacts that should be assessed. The results can be used to support peer judgements for important evaluations or to replace them for less important evaluations. The average number of citations or average indicator score per publication is rarely a good choice for the indicator formula. The reason is that such averages vary greatly by field and year (see Section 9.3) and so comparisons that mix fields and years are unfair. The same is likely to be true for all types of web citations.

If the sets of articles to be assessed were all published in the same field and year, then it would be reasonable to compare the average indicator scores between them. Since sets of citation counts and most web indicator scores seem to be highly skewed, the geometric mean should be used instead of the arithmetic mean for averaging (see Section 9.5).

There are several choices of averaging indicator for collections of documents from multiple fields and/or years. For citation counts, it is standard practice to use a field-normalised average impact indicator, such as the mean normalised citation score (MNCS) (Waltman et al., 2011). This takes into account field and publication year differences and still gives a single figure for a group, with values higher than 1 indicating the extent to which the average number of citations per paper produced by the group is above the world average. Similarly, figures below 1 indicate that the group's outputs attracted fewer citations per paper than the world average (for details, see Section 9.6). This calculation is field normalised to avoid a group having an advantage if it publishes in a high citation specialism. Two preferable variants of this are the geometric mean normalised citation score (gMNCS), which uses geometric means instead of arithmetic means to cope better with highly skewed data sets, and the mean normalized log-transformed citation score (MNLCS), which is the same as the MNCS except calculated on log-transformed indicator scores, again to cope with skewed data (see Section 9.6). These are also likely to be preferable for all types of web citations, for similar reasons.

Another useful indicator is the proportion of outputs that have a non-zero score for a particular indicator (e.g., the proportion of articles that have at least one Mendeley reader). This is valuable when most scores are zero or 1, so all average scores are close to zero and the feature that most distinguishes between two sets of outputs is the proportion that has a non-zero value (Section 9.7). A field-equalised variant of this can be calculated for sets of articles that span multiple fields and/or years (Section 9.7.1), as well as a world-normalised variant, the normalised proportion cited (NPC) (Section 9.8).

The percentage of publications in the top 1% for a field and year, and sometimes top 10% and top 50% is a useful field-independent indicator (Hicks et al., 2015). This can safely be compared between fields and years and the percentages can be averaged between sets of articles from different fields and years to give a field-independent multi-year, multi-field version (Waltman and Schreiber, 2013). Percentiles are currently (August 2016) also used by Altmetric.com for individual articles. For example, it reported that an overall Altmetric.com score of 378 for the article "Biophysical and economic limits to negative CO_2 emissions" was "In the top 5% of all research outputs scored by Altmetric."

All field-normalised and field-independent indicators discussed above need, in theory, a reference set of indicator values for all of the world's outputs in the fields and years examined. This is because the normalisation process requires a world average, and the field-independent percentile indicator needs a complete collection of the world's articles. In practice for traditional citation analysis, articles in a Scopus or WoS subject category are usually used as a proxy for the world's publications in a given field and year. The same strategy can also be adopted for alternative indicators. This can impose a substantial burden on an evaluation because it requires calculating indicator values for (world) publications that are not being assessed. For example, suppose that a research group is judged on its outputs spanning four years and five fields. Assuming that there are 10,000 articles per year and field, then web citation data would be needed for 4 x 5 x 10,000 = 200,000 publications. If it is slow or time consuming to obtain this data, then a random sample of the world's articles may be used instead. For example, a random sample of 500 per field and year for the above research group would reduce the number of articles needed for field normalisation to a more practical 4 x 5 x 500 = 10,000. These could be extracted with relative ease by Webometric Analyst (see Chapter 8 and 10) for most of the indicators discussed in this book.

The recommended overall strategy for collecting indicators for sets of publications is as follows.

1. Decide upon the type of indicators that are relevant to the evaluation (e.g., educational, scholarly or societal impact).

2. Choose the specific indicators needed to assess the types of impact chosen (e.g., syllabus mentions, PowerPoint citations). Alternative indicators that have higher correlations with citations and a higher proportion of non-zero values are preferred, when there is a choice. Spammable indicators must not be used for important evaluations for which advance manipulation would be possible.

3. Gather the raw data for the indicators from a citation database, if citations (e.g., WoS, Scopus, Chinese Social Sciences Citation Index), or from Webometric Analyst for most other indicators (see Chapter 8).

4. Calculate geometric mean indicator averages if all publications are from a single field and year, or MNLCS values if there are multiple fields and/or years using Webometric Analyst (Section 9.6).

5. Calculate the proportion of non-zero values and the NPC world normalised variant for indicators that have few non-zero values, again using Webometric Analyst (Section 9.7.1).

6. For each indicator, calculate 95% confidence intervals so that the statistical significance of any differences between groups can be assessed. Webometric Analyst automatically does this when calculating the indicators.

7. Use human judgement to evaluate the practical significance of the statistically significant differences found between groups. Bear in mind that differences may be due to systematic biases, such as one group publishing most articles in a high citation specialism within a field.

Stages 4–6 above are all carried out by a single step in Webometric Analyst. The final stage, calculating confidence intervals, is important so that minor differences between groups can be ignored as irrelevant.

In summary, field-normalised indicator formulae are needed for comparisons of the impacts of the outputs of sets of departments. Data gathering and formula calculations can be largely automated. If field-normalised web indicators are provided by data providers like Altmetric.com and ImpactStory then this would make them simpler to use for others because each evaluator could buy in the results rather than having to individually repeat the same data gathering and field normalisation process. The top X% indicator of Altmetric.com helps in this regard but is less useful for rare indicators with a high proportion of zeros.

7.5   INSTITUTIONS

The situation above for research groups also applies to institutions (including the proviso about spammable indicators). Since institutions typically support a wide range of academic disciplines, field normalisation is particularly important to ensure that individual departments within the university are not unfairly characterised as contributing low scores to the institution.

Institutions should be cautious when using the basket of metrics approach as a blanket strategy with many indicators. It would be easy to draw false conclusions from this because the number of indicators multiplied by the number of departments would be large enough to ensure that many indicators gave a misleadingly positive (or negative) impression, simply because of random factors in the data (known as the multiple comparisons problem in statistics). In this context, institutions should be aware of the temptation to cherry pick indicators to give a good impression. Because of the influence of random factors, some indicators are likely to give a better impression than others by pure chance. This is the opposite message to that for researchers (Section 7.2), who should cherry pick indicators, but only when they support an impact context that can be explained in their CV or cover letter. The basket of metrics approach may be useful instead to point to areas within the institution that are particularly strong in generating particular types of impacts. For example, if a department has a high level of educational impact then this might be revealed by the education-related indicators in the basket.

A prominent institution-level use of citation indicators is for public international and national university rankings (Waltman et al., 2012). Spammable alternative indicators are inappropriate for these because there are substantial financial incentives for institutions to improve their ranking in any well-known list. When considering indicators for institutions, some of the most well-known university rankings have used (non web) indicators that are not fit for this purpose (Gingras, 2014).

7.6   FUNDING AGENCIES

Research funders may periodically attempt to quantify the success of a particular funding stream or their overall funding programme (Dinsmore et al., 2014; Thelwall et al., 2016). With citations this could be done in various simple ways, such as by assessing the proportion of funded articles in the top journals or top quartile of journals by impact factor.

Field-normalised citation counts and web indicator scores can also be calculated for the funded articles (e.g., MNLCS, see above) to see whether they tend to attract higher values than the world average for the field, following the guidelines at the end of Section 7.4. In this situation, assuming that there are no stakeholders with an interest in any particular evaluation outcome, the possibility of deliberate manipulation is reduced and there is a free choice of indicators. If the funder targets a particular type of impact, then this should drive the choice of indicator but if the funder is interested in any type of impact then a range of different indicators should be used. In this case, as for institutional evaluations, the funder should beware of drawing overly positive conclusions by selecting the indicator that gives the best outcome.

Of particular value for funders conducting a general impact evaluation are Mendeley reader counts because these can provide earlier impact evidence than citations. These are therefore strongly recommended for their ability to give early evidence for programme evaluations. For this, their national and seniority biases (i.e., the dominance of junior researchers) should be taken into account when interpreting the results.

7.7   COUNTRIES

Some countries periodically compare the impact of their research with that of other countries either to assess their current research strength against their international competitors or to monitor changes that are due to new national research policies. Countries are in a similar position to research funding agencies and the recommendations above (Section 7.6) apply. The main difference is one of emphasis: for countries it would be particularly important to calculate a separate field normalised indicator for each of the most recent years so that trends over time can be identified. Interpreting international comparisons is difficult for web indicators because there are national differences in the extent of use of the web and there can be large differences in the uptake of social websites. These differences influence web indicators because there is a natural tendency for people to be more interested in research from their own country, either because they are familiar with the authors or because the topic is more likely to be one of interest within the country. Thus, for example, international differences in the extent to which Mendeley is used makes it difficult to compare Mendeley reader counts between countries that use it to different extents (Fairclough and Thelwall, 2015).

7.8   JOURNALS

Academic publishers often display Journal Impact Factors on journal websites and these seem to be important to many researchers, despite public concerns about their limitations (DORA, 2013). The JIF for an academic journal for a specified year is the number of citations from articles published in that year in all indexed journals to articles published in the previous two years in the given journal, divided by the number of articles published in those two years by that journal. The most recent JIF for a journal represents the average rate of citation of relatively recent articles in the journal (Garfield, 1999), based upon the coverage of the citation database used to calculate it. One of the limitations of the JIF is that it only reflects uses of an article by publishing authors and ignores student and professional readers. It is logical, therefore, to create complementary indicators with a formula that is similar to the JIF but with alternative indicator data instead of traditional citation counts. Another strategy to generate an alternative to the JIF that addresses non-academic uses of articles is to exploit local usage data to create a type of localised usage impact factor. These could help assess the local utility of journals from their downloads (Bollen et al., 2005).

In terms of web indicators, citation counts in the JIF formula have been replaced by social reference sharing site bookmarks (Haustein and Siebenlist, 2011). In addition, using reader categories, it would be possible to generate JIFs for students separately from JIFs for academics. It is also possible to use web data to create JIFs for different impact types. For example, using syllabus mentions, it would be possible to create educational JIFs. Given the importance attached to traditional JIFs by some academics and researchers, however, variants based on web data seem likely to be spammed if used for successful public applications.

7.9   NON-ACADEMIC ORGANISATIONS

Non-academic organisations seeking to evaluate their grey literature may find traditional citation counts to be irrelevant because their work is not aimed at academics but targets policy makers or practitioners instead. For these, alternative indicators carry the promise of giving a type of quantitative impact evidence where previously nothing similar was available, except for media coverage data from organizations such as LexisNexis and ProQuest. Non-academic organisations can opt for the individual approach of Section 7.2 above by making a case for the likely impact of each publication and attempting to support that case with selected alternative indicators. They may instead prefer the group approach to see whether their publications have an impact that is above average overall for their sector.

The group approach described above for academics is not easily transferrable to non-academic organisations because of the need for field normalisation. For this, a comprehensive list of publications categorised by field and year is needed. While this is conveniently provided by both WoS and Scopus, there is no equivalent for the grey literature. Although it would be possible in theory to build a suitable grey literature database for this process, the grey literature is highly varied in size and intended audience and so a more reasonable approach is to benchmark the organisation's outputs against similar outputs from one or more comparable organisations. In this way it is possible to get a very broad impression of whether one organisation's publications are performing better than the other's. For this, unless large numbers of publications (>30) are involved, it makes sense to report the raw indicator values for each publication rather than to calculate averages because the greater transparency of the raw data will allow interpretations to take into account the purposes of the individual documents.

Since non-academic organisations can have highly varied types of impacts from their work, a content analysis of a random sample of the citing sources for any relevant web indicators is recommended in order to characterise the typical type of impacts generated by the organisation's outputs. This content analysis involves human judges reading the random sample of citing sources and categorising them into relevant impact types. The content analysis complements the web indictors gathered by giving context in order to help interpret their meanings.

7.10   RESEARCH ADMINISTRATORS AND MANAGERS

Research administrators and managers can be involved in evaluating individual researchers and making institutional funding decisions. Indicators can be helpful for managing fields when the subject expertise to evaluate individual outputs is lacking. Managers need to be aware that all indicators are partial and biased, however. This means that low web indicator values for individual outputs do not mean low quality or low impact. While researchers should be praised for high values that are likely to be evidence of success, low values should not be used as evidence of failure. Instead, researchers should be asked to provide their own methods of justification for the merits of their work when this is needed. In some cases, this justification might unavoidably be purely qualitative.

7.11   ACADEMIC LIBRARIANS

Librarians can be called upon to help searchers and publishing scholars and therefore Sections 7.1 and 7.2 are particularly relevant for them. In some situations, they may also need to advise research managers and administrators (Section 7.10). Librarians need to know the potential of alternative indicators in order to encourage their use in appropriate cases and also need to know their limitations so that they can advise on the most appropriate interpretations. More detailed information on this is available in other books (Holmberg, 2015; Tattersall, 2016).

7.12   SCHOLARLY COMMUNICATION AND SCIENCE AND TECHNOLOGY STUDIES RESEARCHERS

One of the most promising uses for alternative indicators is for researchers of scholarly communication because these can exploit the new web indicators without fear of deliberate manipulation by stakeholders, and investigate different types of impact, and earlier impact, as a result.

If a study focuses on an emerging research specialism, then the timeliness of most alternative indicators is a particular advantage and Mendeley is recommended for this property in combination with its relative robustness. This robustness is the main advantage of Mendeley over microblogs, which are timelier.

A major advantage of web indicators for scholarly communication researchers is that they can reveal different aspects of scholarly communication and different types of impacts. Depending on the purpose of a study, it may be useful to focus on an individual indicator or a few key indicators. For example, if exploring the educational value of a research area then syllabus, PowerPoint and Wikipedia citations would be the most appropriate.

If a research project needs to access more detailed information about who cites research then systematic quantitative information is available in Mendeley about readers' occupations, geographic locations and disciplines. In contrast, the best qualitative information available will be from science blogs because these typically contain mini reviews of articles, have the most detail, and often are connected to information about the background of the blogger. Science blog posts about academic articles are quite rare and so their prevalence needs to be checked ahead of a study. Microblogs are a compromise approach because they contain some textual information but very few tweets about academic papers give useful details. Most contain the article title or at the most a short summary or highlight (Thelwall et al., 2013b).

A scholarly communication project might also have the goal to understand the role of a new indicator in scholarly communication or to trace related patterns of use amongst scholars. Such studies would help those who use alternative indicators by increasing understanding of their patterns of use.

7.13   SUMMARY

As evident from this chapter, there are many different applications for web indicators. The most visible current one is within digital libraries to aid literature searching. One of the most promising uses is to aid those researching science itself, such as by tracing patterns or influence or identifying differing pathways to impact areas of research. In contrast, the other applications concern formative or summative evaluations of research outputs. Despite this common task, the specifics of an evaluation depend on its purpose and the amount and nature of the outputs being evaluated.

CHAPTER 8

Collecting Data for Sets of Documents

This chapter gives an overview of how to use Webometric Analyst (Figure 8.1) to collect a range of web indicator data for articles, conference papers or books. For individual articles, indicator scores may be found within the publisher's website or from the sites of data providers such as Altmetric. com and ImpactStory. Altmetric.com also provides free downloads of data to researchers and has an API (http://api.altmetric.com/) that can be accessed via Webometric Analyst to download records for sets of articles. Although this chapter mainly deals with extracting indicator data for sets of documents, it is also possible to automatically extract data for non-standard outputs from specific websites using a crawler. Steps to achieve this are explained in Section 8.17. The crawling approach extracts all data from a website rather than values for a specific set of non-standard outputs (e.g., those created by a single research group). So it is more appropriate for research investigations than for specific evaluations.

The Webometric Analyst website (http://lexiurl.wlv.ac.uk) gives detailed step-by-step introductions so the purpose of this chapter is to give an overview of the relevant functions and steps. All of the facilities described here were available when this book was written but some may be withdrawn by the provider at a later date and other indicators may be added. Updates will be made available on the website.

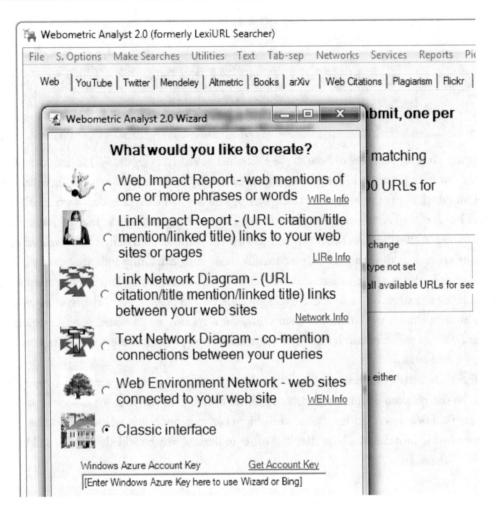

Figure 8.1: A screenshot of Webometric Analyst, showing the start-up wizard above the main interface. At the top of the main interface is a menu bar with a range of different functions, and underneath this is a set of tabs (Web, YouTube, Twitter, Mendeley, Altmetric, Books, arXiv, Web Citations, Plagiarism, Flickr) for collections of related functions.

8.1   OVERVIEW OF WEBOMETRIC ANALYST

Webometric Analyst is a free computer program that runs on Microsoft Windows and is able to collect and process a wide range of types of web indicator data. For most indicators, it must be fed with a list of documents to be assessed, in a format that it understands, and sometimes also a key to access the data on the remote site. The list format is a simple one that separates the document metadata, such as the publication year, authors and title. The indicator data is then usually saved to a file in a simple format that can be processed in a spreadsheet like Excel. Webometric Analyst is designed to automate operations that would take a long time to do manually so that it is possible to gather indicator data for larger sets of documents.

Webometric Analyst can be downloaded from http://lexiurl.wlv.ac.uk/ and updates are posted to the site every few months to fix bugs or to add extra features. This site also contains on-line instructions for using its main features. Not all of its features are documented because many of them are simple, rarely use, or best understood by trying them out.

The two main features offered by Webometric Analyst are the ability to download web indicator data and a large set of functions for processing the data downloaded by it or its sister web crawler, SocSciBot. Webometric Analyst extracts information from websites through their APIs when they allow free data harvesting. In some cases, users must register for either the API (e.g., Bing) or for the website itself (e.g., Mendeley, Twitter) and then enter a key or PIN in order to give Webometric Analyst permission to use the API. Information about this process is given on the software website or through prompts within the program.

Some of the indicator data needs a three-stage process to collect: creating the file of document information for the set to be assessed, using Webometric Analyst to create appropriate Bing queries, and then running the Bing queries with Webometric Analyst (Figure 8.2, left). Mendeley and Twitter data collection do not need Bing and have instead a more direct two-step process (Figure 8.2, right).

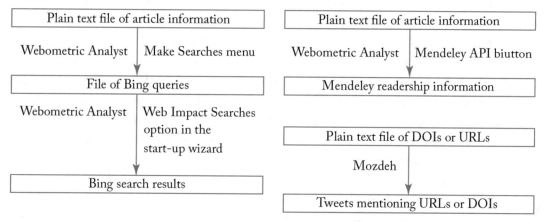

Figure 8.2: The three-stage process needed to generate the indicator values for patents, syllabus mentions, web citations, blog citations and grey literature citations (when Bing queries are needed—left), the two stages for Mendeley readers (top right) and the two stages with Mozdeh when tweets are needed (bottom right).

This chapter describes how to gather raw web indicator data and Chapter 10 describes how to use this raw data to calculate averages, proportions and field-normalised indicators.

8.1.1   THE BING API

The Bing API allows automatic web searches using the Bing search engine. This API makes it possible to gather many web indicators that are based on web searching, including syllabus citations, patent citations and grey literature citations. From December 2016 the Bing API will have a limited trial use free version (currently allowing 1,000 operations per month for three months) and a paid upgrade, allowing more operations at a small cost. Although the API rate per query is low (e.g., $3 per month to Microsoft for up to 1,000 queries at the time of writing), the total cost may be prohibitive for large-scale uses. It is important to read the terms and conditions carefully when signing up and remember to cancel the key as soon as it is no longer needed because the charging is automatic and continues even if the API is not used. Information about signing up for the Bing API is available on the Webometric Analyst website.

8.2   FORMATTING SETS OF JOURNAL ARTICLES FOR WEBOMETRIC ANALYST

Webometric Analyst always uses a simple plain text file format for its input and usually uses a similar format for the results. In a few cases, the input file will be a list of pre-formed queries and these are always entered in a plain text file, with exactly one query on each line. Plain text files are simplest to create in the Windows Notepad program that can be found within the Accessories Windows program group. Some other software, such as Microsoft Word, allow their files to be converted to this plain text format (select Save As from the file menu ribbon and choose Plain text (*.txt) from the list of file formats) but may render the file useless by saving unwanted characters (e.g., smart quotes or apostrophes instead of straight quotes or apostrophes). They may also add extra blank data that is not visible in Notepad but causes Webometric Analyst to malfunction, such as extra tab characters when saving from Microsoft Excel. Thus, the use of these is only recommended for brave experts on file formatting issues.

The most common file format used by Webometric Analyst for input files is tab-separated plain text (Figure 8.3). With this format, each reference is on a separate line. Within each line, the key components of the reference are separated by a tab. For example, each line of a file might contain the information:

```
Title<tab>Publication year<tab>Author names<tab>Pub-
lishing journal<tab>DOI
```

Figure 8.3 illustrates a few lines of data in the above format, viewed in Windows Notepad.

```
Figure 11.1.txt - Notepad
File  Edit  Format  View  Help
Author(s)      Year    Title   Publication     Doi
Geller T.      2013    Is film theory queer theory?    Camera Obscura  10.1215/02705346-2352243
Richards J.    2013    Berlin Alexanderplatz's serial women    Camera Obscura  10.1215/02705346-2352158
Nichols J.     2013    Cinemactivism: Film reform, spectatorship, and the Cleveland Cinema Club        Ca
Fischer L.     2013    Afterlife and afterimage: Maya Deren in \"transfigured time\"   Camera Obscura  1(
McBean S.      2013    Seeing in Alison Bechdel's fun home     Camera Obscura  10.1215/02705346-2352167
```

Figure 8.3: A Notepad file with journal article information separated by tabs. The tabs do not align the columns because the titles have different lengths.

If every line of a file is in exactly the same format, Webometric Analyst can easily identify and separate out the different components of the references in order to build its queries. If many of the above rows are entered into a document, then some of them will align into neat columns and others will not but this does not matter as long as there is a single tab between each component of each reference. It is very time consuming to create the above format, although it can be done manually with Windows Notepad, but it is better to create it in a spreadsheet like Excel or, if saving data from the Web of Science or Scopus, choose their option to save in tab-separated plain text format (see lexiurl.wlv.ac.uk/reports/ for specific instructions).

If creating the file in a spreadsheet, then each reference should be entered into a single row and each part of the reference should be entered into the same column. For example, the title might always be in column C and the publication year or date in column B. Figure 8.4 gives an example.

	A	B	C	D	E
1	**Author(s)**	**Date**	**Title**	**Publication**	**Doi**
2	Geller T.	31/12/2013	Is film theory queer theory? Or, everyt	Camera Obscura	10.1215/02705346-2352243
3	Richards J.	31/12/2013	Berlin Alexanderplatz's serial women	Camera Obscura	10.1215/02705346-2352158
4	Nichols J.	31/12/2013	Cinemactivism: Film reform, spectator	Camera Obscura	10.1215/02705346-2352149
5	Fischer L.	31/12/2013	Afterlife and afterimage: Maya Deren i	Camera Obscura	10.1215/02705346-2352139
6	McBean S.	31/12/2013	Seeing in Alison Bechdel's fun home	Camera Obscura	10.1215/02705346-2352167

Figure 8.4: A spreadsheet with document information separated into columns.

The file formats used by spreadsheets cannot be read by Webometric Analyst and so the file must be saved in ta-separated plain text format. In Microsoft Excel, select Save As from the File menu ribbon and choose Text (tab delimited) from the list of file formats. If this creates smart quotes or smart apostrophes, then these should be replaced with their straight counterparts. This can be achieved by opening the file in Windows Notepad and using the Replace All command to replace the smart version (copy and paste it from the document) with the straight version (type it in using the keyboard). The spreadsheet might save extra blank columns and rows but this should not make any difference to Webometric Analyst, which will ignore them.

8.3   FORMATTING SETS OF BOOKS FOR WEBOMETRIC ANALYST

For processing by Webometric Analyst, a tab-delimited plain text file of the information for each book is needed, similar to that needed for journal articles and with one book per line. The main difference is that books have ISBNs rather than DOIs so the DOI column is replaced with an ISBN column, if needed for the indicator collected. ISBNs are required for some of the web indicators but not others, and some indicators only need ISBNs. If the books are extracted from Scopus or WoS then saving them directly into tab-delimited plain text files should be sufficient.

Within each line, the key components of the reference are separated by a tab. For example, each line of a file might contain this information (the ISBN information can be omitted for most indicators):

Author(s)<tab>Title<tab>Year<tab>Publisher<tab>ISBN

Figure 8.5 illustrates some data in the above format, omitting the ISBN column, viewed in Windows Notepad.

Figure 8.5: A Notepad file with book information separated by tabs. The tabs do not align the columns because the sections have different lengths.

8.4   MENDELEY READERS

To collect Mendeley readership data for a set of articles, either the article DOIs are needed in a simple plain text file format (one DOI per line) or the metadata (author names, title, journal name, publication year) should be saved into a tab-separated plain text file format, as described above. If possible, a DOI column should also be included in the latter case so that Webometric Analyst can use the DOIs, when available, to check matches and find additional matches (Zahedi et al., 2014b). Not all records in Mendeley have DOIs, even if the associated articles do, and so including the extra information described above in addition to the DOI allows Webometric Analyst to search for additional matches. The following illustrates a Mendeley query that was automatically generated by Webometric Analyst from the title, author and publication year of a journal article, ignoring its DOI.

```
title:Optical coherence tomography Significance of a
new method for assessing unclear laryngeal pathologies
AND author:Glanz AND year:2010
```

In Mendeley, some articles have multiple records and Webometric Analyst takes care of combining the results for all correct matches for any article. The matching process is imperfect, so it sometimes makes mistakes. Problems include Mendeley readers entering incorrect article information, articles having multiple valid titles (e.g., in different languages) and titles containing accented characters or mathematical symbols that may be entered in different ways. These issues may be a particular problem if a collection of articles has a mathematical orientation or includes a substantial number of texts in languages that use non-ASCII or accented characters.

Although books do not often seem to be entered into Mendeley, they can be searched for on the site using their author name, publication year and title. The procedure is otherwise the same as for journal articles

Webometric Analyst gathers data via the free Mendeley API. This is a programming interface that allows the automatic harvesting of data. In order to use the API via Webometric Analyst it is essential to sign up as a Mendeley user first. When running Mendeley queries, Webometric Analyst will ask for a key that can be obtained by logging in to Mendeley. The procedure is as follows (following the top of the right hand side of Figure 8.2).

1. Save the metadata for the articles in the tab-delimited format described in Section 8.2, including either DOIs or article titles, authors and publication years, or both.

2. Start Webometric Analyst, close down the start-up wizard, select the *Mendeley* tab from the main (classic) interface, click the *Search For Publications* button and select the plain text file created by step 1.

Mendeley gives a lot of information about each article that has readers, and not just the total number of readers. It reports the number of readers by country, field and occupation. These three figures are only provided for Mendeley members that have entered such information, which is often not all of them. This information is therefore about a sample of the Mendeley readership rather than all Mendeley readers. In addition, the information may be out of date if a member forgets to change it when she gets promoted, changes specialism, completes her Ph.D. or moves to another country. Nevertheless, it seems reasonable to use the data as a very rough guideline. Even if information is out of date, it might have been correct at the time when the user entered a specific reference into the site.

The format of the Mendeley data is a huge file in the simple tab-delimited format that can be copied into, or opened by, a spreadsheet to be read (Figure 8.6). The first columns of the spreadsheet replicate the data inputted into Webometric Analyst and the remaining columns give the new information supplied by Mendeley. The specialism, country and occupation columns are likely to be very sparse—mainly blanks with only a few entries. Webometric Analyst only reports the countries and specialisms within the data so missing countries have no readers.

Authors	Readers	PhDStudent	StudentMaster	StudentBachelor
Wang, Xiaofei	12	3	1	0
Hu, Yong; Fen	17	1	1	0
Mustafa, Muh	0	0	0	0
Lee, Junghoor	5	1	0	0
Hughes-Halle	7	1	0	0
Lubowiecka, I	5	1	0	0
Ercan, Burak; I	1	0	0	0
Zverovich, Va	1	0	0	0
Yang, Hongxia	0	0	0	0

Figure 8.6: A spreadsheet showing some information returned by the Mendeley API, separated into columns and with one row per publication.

8.5   GREY LITERATURE CITATIONS

Grey literature can appear on many different websites but can be found using search engine queries exploiting the filetype: advanced search command and combining it with document metadata, such as the authors, title and publication year. This process can be automated in Webometric Analyst using the Bing API. It consumes a minimum of two Bing API queries per document, one for each file type searched for (Word and PDF). The procedure for collecting grey literature citations follows the left hand side of Figure 8.2.

1. Save the metadata for the documents in the tab-delimited format described in Section 8.2 or 8.3.

2. Start Webometric Analyst, close the start-up wizard and select the *Make grey literature searches for a set of Scopus/WoS/Other journal articles or books* option from the *Make Searches* menu to create a set of Bing queries for these articles in a standard format. As described in Section 4.5, each article will have two queries, both containing the first few words of the article title in quotes, the first author last name and publication year, together with either the filetype:pdf or the filetype:doc command at the end.

3. Restart Webometric Analyst, enter the Bing API key (see Section 8.1.1), select the web impact report option in the start-up wizard and choose the plain text file of queries generated by step 2.

8.5.1 STANDARD WEBOMETRIC ANALYST RESULTS REPORTS

Webometric Analyst produces results in several different forms. Although the simplest output is a plain text file listing the number of matches for each query submitted, it also produces a more informative set of webpages that form a mini report. In this set of webpages there is a table of results as well as a list of matching URLs for each query. The tables include not only the total number of URLs returned for each query but also the number of different domain names, websites and top-level domains (TLDs) within these results (Figures 8.7, 8.8, 8.9). The *domain-level results are recommended rather than the URL-level results* when it is possible that some websites contain multiple copies of pages so that web citations can be double-counted.

For the URLs http://www.scit.wlv.ac.uk/~cm1993/mycv.html and http://www.umass.edu/afroam/thelwellnew.htm this is the meaning of the terms used in the reports:

- **URL:** The complete webpage URL.

- **Domain:** The domain name part of the URL after the initial :// and before the first slash after it (e.g., www.scit.wlv.ac.uk and www.umass.edu).

- **Site:** The end of the domain name part of the URL. This is the part after the penultimate dot if there isn't a category naming segment. If there is a category segment, then an extra segment is included. This typically describes the website of an entire organisation, even if it is split into different domains (e.g., wlv.ac.uk because ac is the academic segment of the uk domain, and umass.edu because .edu does not use the segmenting system).

- **STLD:** For websites with a category segment before the TLD, this is the category name plus the TLD, otherwise it is the TLD (e.g., ac.uk and edu).

- **TLD**: The final segment of the domain name, after the last dot (e.g., uk and edu).

Table listing the URLs of pages matching the queries submitted. In addition, it contains the number of domains, sites, STLDs and TLDs containing one or more URL matching the query, as derived from the URL list.

Name	Base query	URLs	Domains	Sites	STLDs	TLDs
-	"Academic Tribes and Territories" Becher 2001 filetype:pdf|"Academic Tribes and Territories" Becher 2001 filetype:doc	323	**257**	220	53	45
-	"The intellectual and social organization of the sciences" Whitley 2000 filetype:pdf|"The intellectual and social organization of the sciences" Whitley 2000 filetype:doc	66	**59**	58	25	24
-	"The Professional Quest for Truth: A Social Theory of Science and Knowledge" fuchs 1992 filetype:pdf|"The Professional Quest for Truth: A Social Theory of Science and Knowledge" fuchs 1992 filetype:doc	12	**10**	10	6	6
-	"The Sociology of Science" Merton 1973 filetype:pdf|"The Sociology of Science" Merton 1973 filetype:doc	646	**531**	436	67	59

*Definitions of terms. Note that the **bold** column is the most reliable.*

- URLs - the number of URLs returned by the search engine (NOT the estimated number of URLs it reports)
- Domains - the domain names of the URLs matching the query
- Sites - the distinguishing end of the domain names of the URLs matching the query (e.g., microsoft.com, ox.ac.uk, w3.org, yahoo.co.uk - it is always the SLD plus one extra section on the left)
- STLD - the second level domain (when existing, otherwise the top level domain) of the URLs matching the query (e.g., .com, .ac.uk, .edu, .co.nz)
- TLD - the top level domain of the URLs matching the query (e.g., .com, .uk, .edu, .nz)

Figure 8.7: A Webometric Analyst table reporting the results of a search for grey literature mentioning any one of four books. The domains column is recommended for indicators rather than the URLs column because of the possibility of duplicate URLs for the same page.

Domain	URLs	%
link.springer.com	2	16.7%
www.scit.wlv.ac.uk	2	16.7%
sociology.arizona.edu	1	8.3%
www.journals.uchicago.edu	1	8.3%
www.tandfonline.com	1	8.3%
www.personal.kent.edu	1	8.3%
muse.jhu.edu	1	8.3%
researchonline.jcu.edu.au	1	8.3%
uwaterloo.ca	1	8.3%
anet.ua.ac.be	1	8.3%

Figure 8.8: The list of web domains extracted from the list of URLs of grey literature pages mentioning *The professional quest for truth*.

TLD	Domains	%
edu	119	22.4%
org	58	10.9%
com	47	8.9%
ru	30	5.6%
uk	25	4.7%
ca	21	4.0%
de	20	3.8%
fr	19	3.6%
net	16	3.0%
nl	11	2.1%
it	11	2.1%
es	9	1.7%

Figure 8.9: TLDs extracted from the list of URLs of grey literature pages mentioning *The sociology of science*. Most of the literature is from U.S. universities (which dominate .edu) but there are also many websites from Russia (.ru) and the UK (.uk).

The above data can be copied and pasted into a spreadsheet for analysis or the files could be used as the input for Webometric Analyst to apply indicator formulae (Chapter 10).

8.6   PATENT CITATIONS

Patent citations on the Google Patents website can be searched for via the Bing API because Bing indexes the Google Patents website. For this, Webometric Analyst's Make Searches menu can be used to convert a tab-delimited plain text file (as in Section 8.2 or 8.3) into a new plain text file that contains queries built from the publication title, year and first author name, combined with the site: advanced search command site:google.com/patents to restrict the results to patents indexed by Google. This file can be run using the Web Impact Report option of the Webometric Analyst start-up wizard, producing tab-delimited plain text files and lists of matching patents. The procedure follows the left hand side of Figure 8.2.

1. Save the metadata for the documents in the tab-delimited format described in Section 8.2 or 8.3.

2. Start Webometric Analyst, close the start-up wizard, select the *Make Google Patent searches for a set of Scopus/WoS/Other journal articles or books* option from the *Make Searches* menu to create a set of Bing queries for these articles. Each article query will contain the

first few words of the article title in quotes, the first author last name and publication year, together with the site:google.com/patents command at the end.

3. Restart Webometric Analyst, enter the Bing API key (see Section 8.1.1), select the web impact report option in the start-up wizard and choose the plain text file of queries generated by step 2.

The results are saved in a standard set of reports, as described in Section 8.5.1.

8.7   POWERPOINT CITATIONS

This is almost the same as for grey literature citations, except for the document type searched for and the use of only one query per document.

1. Save the metadata for the documents in the tab-delimited format described in Section 8.2 or 8.3.

2. Start Webometric Analyst, close the start-up wizard, select the *Make PowerPoint searches for a set of Scopus/WoS/Other journal articles or books* option from the *Make Searches* menu to create a set of Bing queries for these articles. As described in Section 5.2, each article query will contain the first few words of the article title in quotes, the first author last name and publication year, together with the filetype:ppt command at the end.

3. Restart Webometric Analyst, enter the Bing API key (Section 8.1.1), select the web impact report option in the start-up wizard and choose the plain text file of queries from step 2.

The results are saved in a standard set of reports, as described in Section 8.5.1.

8.8   WIKIPEDIA CITATIONS

This is the same as for patent citations, except with the Wikipedia website instead of the Google Patents website.

1. Save the metadata for the documents in the tab-delimited format described in Section 8.2 or 8.3.

2. Start Webometric Analyst, close the start-up wizard, select the *Make Wikipedia searches for a set of Scopus/WoS/Other journal articles or books* option from the *Make Searches* menu to create a set of Bing queries for these articles. As described in Section 5.3, each article query will contain the first few words of the article title in quotes, the first author last

name and publication year, together with the site:wikipedia.org/wiki/ command at the end.

3. Restart Webometric Analyst, enter the Bing API key (Section 8.1.1), select the web impact report option in the start-up wizard and choose the plain text file of queries from step 2.

   The results are saved in a standard set of reports, as described in Section 8.5.1.

8.9   BLOG CITATIONS

There is no fool-proof way to search for webpages that are blogs and exclude those that are not. In this situation, heuristics are needed. Webometric Analyst searches a list of major blog sites in order to identify their blogs, but cannot identify blogs that are not in these major sites. The procedure follows the left hand side of Figure 8.2. It consumes multiple Bing API queries, a minimum of one for each blog site, and so can be expensive.

1. Save the metadata for the documents in the tab-delimited format described in Section 8.2 or 8.3.

2. Start Webometric Analyst, close the start-up wizard, select the *Make major blog (or other site) searches for a set of Scopus/WoS/Other journal articles or books* option from the *Make Searches* menu to create a set of Bing queries for these articles. Each article will have multiple queries, each containing the first few words of the article title in quotes, the first author last name and publication year, together with the site:BLOG command at the end, where BLOG is one of the major blog sites (e.g., blogspot.com, wordpress.com, typepad.com, livejournal.com, scienceblogs.com). The list of blog sites suggested by Webometric Analyst can be changed—for example to remove all except scienceblogs.com)

3. Restart Webometric Analyst, enter the Bing API key (Section 8.1.1), select the web impact report option in the start-up wizard and choose the plain text file of queries from step 2.

   The results are saved in a standard set of reports, as described in Section 8.5.1.

8.10   SYLLABUS CITATIONS

Searching for syllabus citations online is more complex than searching for most other types of indicator because the queries for online syllabi are not very accurate and so the results need to be filtered after they have been obtained from Bing. The procedure follows the left hand side of Figure 8.2 to start with.

1. Save the metadata for the documents in the tab-delimited format described in Section 8.2 or 8.3.

2. Start Webometric Analyst, close the start-up wizard, select the *Make syllabus searches for a set of Scopus/WoS/Other journal articles or books* option from the *Make Searches* menu to create a set of Bing queries for these articles. As described in Section 5.1, each article will have two queries, both containing the first few words of the article title in quotes, the first author last name and publication year, together with either "syllabus" or "course description" at the end.

3. Restart Webometric Analyst, enter the Bing API key (Section 8.1.1), select the web impact report option in the start-up wizard and choose the plain text file of queries generated by step 2.

4. Select the *Syllabus mentions: Filter out from long results* option of the *Utilities* menu and select the long results file generated by the syllabus searches (i.e., the file with "long results" within its filename).

5. From the *Reports* menu, select *Make a set of standard impact reports from a long results file* and choose the filtered syllabus long results file.

The results of the Bing searches using the syllabus query file (step 3) will be a set of URLs that match the queries but that are not necessarily academic syllabi. The purpose of step 4 is to filter out non-syllabi using a predefined set of filtering heuristics. These rules, which can be customised, specify for example, that page URLs or descriptions containing the term *Acquisition* should be removed because they are likely to be library acquisition information rather than syllabus listings.

8.11   GENERAL WEB CITATIONS

The procedure follows the left hand side of Figure 8.2. This is likely to produce many irrelevant matches from library listings and journal contents page listings and so, if possible, it would be useful to add a section to the query to exclude a phrase at the start of each article's abstract. This is an option in Webometric Analyst when making these queries (step 2 below).

1. Save the metadata for the documents in the tab-delimited format described in Section 8.2 or 8.3.

2. Start Webometric Analyst, close the start-up wizard, select the *Make Web searches for a set of Scopus/WoS/Other journal articles or books* option from the *Make Searches* menu to create a set of Bing queries for these articles. Each article query will contain the first few words of the article title in quotes, the first author last name and publication year.

3. Restart Webometric Analyst, enter the Bing API key (see Section 8.1.1), select the web impact report option in the start-up wizard and choose the plain text file of queries generated by step 2.

The results are saved in a standard set of reports, as described in Section 8.5.1.

8.12   TWEET MENTIONS VIA DOIS OR LINKS

Twitter provides a free API that Mozdeh (a free partner tool to Webometric Analyst) can use to search for tweets mentioning an article but there are two complications. First, tweets are not long enough to comfortably contain full citations so articles are usually cited in tweets via a link to the online page for the article or by mentioning the article DOI. In the former case, a list of URLs of the publisher pages for the articles in a collection is needed, which is not straightforward to obtain. If only DOIs are used, then most article mentions will probably be lost. This is a tricky problem with no simple solution with Mozdeh. In most cases, the value of the data gathered would not justify the considerable effort needed to gather tweets in this way.

A second problem is that the query results returned by Twitter are restricted to the previous two weeks, so all older citations will be lost. This can be solved by monitoring Twitter continuously over a long period of time but Twitter citations from more than two weeks before the start date will be lost. For most evaluations, this approach is unlikely to be possible. The alternative is to obtain the Twitter citation counts from an altmetric service provider such as Altmetric.com or ImpactStory. These monitor Twitter continuously and so can deliver the necessary data on demand to their own users. The procedure is as follows.

1. Download Mozdeh from http://mozdeh.wlv.ac.uk and save to a Microsoft Windows computer.

2. Create a list of article DOIs (or article URLs) and save it in a Windows Notepad plain text file, with one per line.

3. Start Mozdeh, enter a name in the new project name box and click the *Start New Project* button.

4. In the new Data Collection window (Figure 8.10), click the *Keep Searching Until Button Clicked* option, click the *Run Twitter Searches in File Continually* button and select the plain text list of article DOIs (or URLs). If desired, also select a given language for the tweets.

5. Follow the instructions given by Mozdeh to get permission from Twitter for the searches.

6. When the desired data collection period (e.g., a few weeks) has completed, click the Stop Monitoring button, which will appear when the monitoring starts.

7. Once the monitoring has finished, load the results file (found in the *raw data* subfolder of the Mozdeh project folder) into a spreadsheet to count the number of matches for each query.

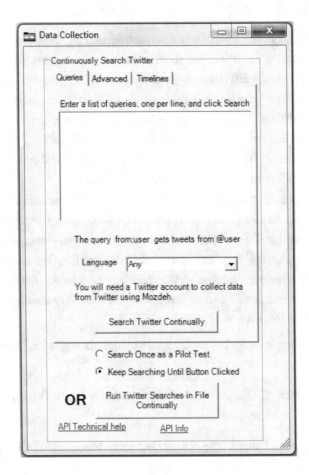

Figure 8.10: The Data Collection window of Mozdeh, showing the Keep Searching Until Button Clicked option checked (near the bottom) and the Run Twitter Searches in File Continually button (also near the bottom). The main blank box and tabs are not needed here.

8.13   GOOGLE BOOKS CITATION COUNTS

Google Books has an API that is used by Webometric Analyst to search for references within the indexed books. The main columns needed in the tab-delimited plain text file for this are the author, title and publication year.

A common problem with books is that different monographs can have the same publication information, especially if they have a short title. In such cases it is impossible to identify which of the two books has been cited each time. In this situation it is best to remove both books completely from the data set and so Webometric Analyst provides a second query file with all duplicate queries completely removed.

The Google Books API returns approximate matches in addition to exact matches and so after getting lists of matching books from the Google Books API the next stage is to filter out the inexact and unwanted matches (e.g., the book itself, advertising lists in other books). This is achieved by another button click in Webometric Analyst (Figure 8.11). The overall procedure is as follows.

1. Save the metadata for the books in the tab-delimited format described in Section 8.3.

2. Start Webometric Analyst, close the start-up wizard and select the Books tab.

3. Within the books tab, click the *1. Make Google Books Queries from Scopus, WoS or Other Data* button and select the tab-delimited file.

4. Click the *2. Search Google Books with all Queries in File* button and follow the instructions. This submits the queries to the Google Book Search API and may take several hours.

5. Click the *3. Remove GBS Matches Without Query Terms* button. This filters out the unwanted Google Books Search matches (see Figure 8.12).

6. Click the *4. Add Filtered GBS Matches to Original Results File* button and follow the instructions. This adds up all the Google Books citations for each book and adds the sum to the original unfiltered (i.e., including the unwanted matches) results file. This gives a file with overall Google Books citation counts for each book.

7. [optional] Click the *5. Add Citation Column to GBS Summary* button and follow the instructions. This adds citation data from another source to the Google Books Search results. This is only if a separate source of citation data is available.

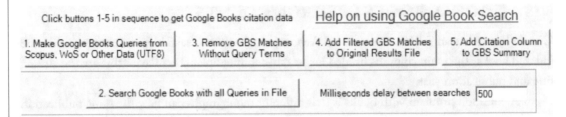

Figure 8.11: The Webometric Analyst buttons illustrating the sequence of operations needed to run Google Books searches.

Name	Date modified	Type	Size
Monographs_gbs searchesNodup_res_matching 4 query terms.txt	29/06/2016 08:59	Text Document	3 KB
Monographs_gbs searchesNodup_res.txt	29/06/2016 08:58	Text Document	10 KB
Monographs_gbs searchesNodup.txt	29/06/2016 08:57	Text Document	1 KB
Monographs.txt	29/06/2016 08:16	Text Document	1 KB

```
Monographs_gbs searchesNodup_res_matching 4 query terms.txt - Notepad

File  Edit  Format  View  Help

Query   ID      Updated Title   DC:Title      DC:Creator     DC:Date DC:Description
DC:Subject
Trimmer "How to Avoid Huge Ships" "Cornell Maritime Press" 1993        http://www.goo
AeAQAAMAAJ      2016-06-29T07:58:21.000Z       Proceedings of the ... Annual Conferen
Annual Conference       Canadian Transportation Research Forum. Conference      2002
Huge Ships, 2nd ed., Cornell Maritime  Press, Centreville, MD, 1993, pp. 3, 15 and 48.
Commission on the Future of the Toronto 14 M.C. Ircha 300.      book           Transp
Trimmer "How to Avoid Huge Ships" "Cornell Maritime Press" 1993
http://www.google.com/books/feeds/volumes/p_U5hbmYJJgC  2016-06-29T07:58:21.000Z
2005    64 2003 &lt;SciRR&gt; Began in 1922. Latest issue consulted: 64th ed. Trimmer,
ed. Centreville, Md., Cornell Maritime Press,  c1993. 99 p. VK371.T74 1993 CONFERENCES
 ...        25 pages25 pages; book         ...     ... Navigation
```

Figure 8.12: A Google Books search results file after clicking Button 3 to filter out bad matches. The tabs do not align the columns because the sections have different lengths.

8.14   WORLDCAT LIBRARY HOLDINGS

Webometric Analyst uses the WorldCat Search API to calculate the number of libraries holding a copy of any book, but this requires permission to be granted first. The first stage for harvesting WorldCat library holdings is to request an API key for the WorldCat Search API from the OCLC webpage at http://www.oclc.org/developer/develop/web-services/worldcat-search-api. en.html. Since they kindly provide the API free of charge and it is mainly intended for librarians, such a request should only be placed for important applications to avoid overusing their services. If granted, the request may take several months to be approved and will then result in a long string of characters which is the API key that must be entered into Webometric Analyst when using it to count library holdings.

The input file should be in plain text or tab-delimited plain text format in which one of the columns contains book ISBNs—this is the only data needed (Figure 8.13). Only one further step is needed.

1. Save a list of ISBNs for the books, one per line, in a Windows Notepad plain text file. The plain text file may also be a tab-delimited file in which one column contains the ISBNs (see Section 8.3).

2. Start Webometric Analyst, close down the start-up wizard and select *WorldCat: Get book holdings from ISBNs* from the *Services* menu and select the plain text file.

The result file echoes the input file with a new column containing the number of libraries holding a copy of each book. This can be loaded into a spreadsheet to analyse or used to calculate indicator formulae, as described in Chapter 10.

```
Example list of book ISBNs_holdings.txt - Notepad
File   Edit   Format   View   Help
InputISBN          Holdings
9783527405978      201
9783527406234      263
9783527290604      312
9783527317868      328
9783527315109      222
9783527313075      455
9783527406708      217
```

Figure 8.13: The WorldCat search results obtained from a list of ISBNs. The Holdings column reports the number of libraries with a copy of each book.

8.15   AMAZON REVIEWS, RATINGS AND SALES RANKS

Although Amazon has an API that can retrieve information about books (its Product Advertising API), it can only be used for marketing books and not for research. Instead, Amazon book information can be extracted from book pages crawled from Amazon.com but first the correct Amazon.com page must be identified for each book. There is an indirect way to identify book pages but a three-stage process is needed for this that starts with automatic search engine searches and includes a manual checking stage.

Identifying Amazon.com book page URLs: A site-specific Bing search of Amazon is needed to identify the correct book page. This should contain the book title, the terms ISBN-10 and ISBN-13 (to ensure that matching pages contain book information) and author last name, as follows. The advanced search site: command is used to restrict the results to the Amazon website.

```
Hoover "How to Live with an Idiot" ISBN-10: ISBN-13:
site:www.amazon.com
```

A plain text file with the required queries can be created with the option *Make Amazon book page searches* in the Webometric Analyst *Make Searches* menu. These queries can be submitted to Bing via its API using the *Run All Searches in File* button in the main tab of the main window (i.e., the classic interface), after entering a Bing API key in the start-up wizard. This button produces a set of files, including one with "long results" within its filename. The long results file should contain the relevant Amazon.com page URL for most books but needs to be manually checked in a spreadsheet to remove any false or duplicate matches. After this manual checking, the URLs of the books should be copied from the relevant column to Windows Notepad and then saved to a plain text file with one URL per line.

Crawling the book pages: The book pages can be crawled with SocSciBot (see Section 8.17), using the plain text file of URLs generated as above.

Extracting book information from the crawled book pages: The Books tab within Webometric Analyst's main (classic) interface contains a button, *Get Amazon Book Info. From Saved Pages*, which can be used to extract the review information about the books in the crawled pages. After clicking on this button, select the root folder from the SocSciBot project containing the crawled pages (see Section 8.17.1). The book information will be saved in a tab-delimited plain text file that can be opened within a spreadsheet program.

8.16   GOODREADS REVIEWS

Goodreads has a free API (www.goodreads.com/api) to enable book reviews and ratings to be automatically extracted for books from their ISBNs. *Webometric Analyst* uses this API and just needs a plain text file of book ISBNs as input.

1. Save a list of ISBNs for the books, one per line, in a Windows Notepad plain text file (see Section 8.3).

2. Start Webometric Analyst, close down the start-up wizard and select the *Books* tab in the main (classic) interface. Click the *Get Goodreads Reviews Stats From ISBNs* button in the Books tab and select the plain text file.

This produces a file of information that can be loaded into a spreadsheet to analyse or processed by Webometric Analyst to calculate indicators (see Chapter 10).

8.17   EXTRACTING DATA FROM WEBSITES VIA SOCSCIBOT CRAWLS

Some websites contain data that is useful for indicator development but do not have an API to access it automatically. These sites can sometimes be mined using automated Bing searches (e.g., for Google patents and Wikipedia) but this is not always possible. In some other cases the website owner allows their site to be crawled and indicator data can be extracted from the crawled pages. While the first step can be carried out with many different free web crawlers, the second step requires a specially written parser that understands the structure of the pages in the crawled site. Some parsers useful for alternative indicators are built into Webometric Analyst.

8.17.1 WEB CRAWLING

A web crawler is a program that can be fed with one or more starting URLs and then recursively downloads the webpages at these URLs and extracts and follows their hyperlinks. The web crawlers that are used to feed commercial search engines try to find a large proportion of the web but for research purposes, crawlers may focus on a single website or part of a website. As long as a website has systematic links between pages then it should be possible to point a research crawler at the start page of a website and then leave it to find all pages in the site, stopping when it has finished.

SocSciBot (http://socscibot.wlv.ac.uk) is an example of a free web crawler and is recommended here because it saves webpages in a simple format that can be processed by Webometric Analyst. The web crawler SocSciBot can be pointed at the home page of a website or fed with a list of page URLs to crawl. By default, SocSciBot crawls one website at a time so if it finds a link to a website that is different from the one that it is crawling then it ignores it.

When crawling a site, it is important to follow ethical guidelines in order to avoid damaging the target site or crawling when it is unwanted. The first main rule to follow is to avoid pages that are marked as off limits to crawlers. SocSciBot, like all ethical crawlers, does this by reading the warning file (always called robots.txt and stored in the root folder of a website) and obeying its restrictions. In order to avoid damaging a site by using up its time with too frequent requests for pages, SocSciBot by default crawls a maximum of one page per second. This means that large sites can take a long time to crawl because the maximum number of pages crawlable in a day is 24x60x60=86,400 and even a small university site could take a week to crawl at this rate. A crawler needs a computer that is left switched on for as long as it takes to complete the crawl. SocSciBot saves the crawled pages to individual files in a simple format that can be parsed by Webometric Analyst to extract indicator data (Figure 8.14).

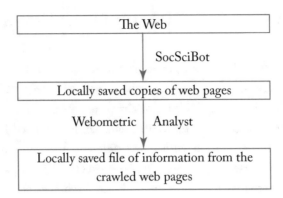

Figure 8.14: The crawling/extraction process. First, SocSciBot crawls webpages, then Webometric Analyst extracts relevant information from the saved pages.

Some websites have an index, called a site map, which lists all pages in the site. The location of such a sitemap is often recorded within the robots.txt file at the root of the site. An alternative way to crawl a site is to locate the site map, extract all the URLs from it, and then use these URLs as the start-up list for SocSciBot. For sites that are too big to crawl (>900,000 pages) a random sample could be crawled instead. To do this, extract the URLs into a single file (this is the tricky part, but can be achieved through Webometric Analyst, after downloading the sitemap file(s), with the *SiteMap XML: Extract all URLs* option in the *Services* menu) and then use the Webometric Analyst option to select a fixed number of lines randomly from the file (*Randomly select n lines in file* from the *Copy* submenu of the *Text* menu). To use this start list, before clicking the *Crawl* button in SocSciBot, check the *Preload start list* box and select the file of random URLs.

Sometimes only part of a website needs to be crawled and this can be specified in SocSciBot by entering the part of the URL that all crawled pages should contain in the second yellow text box (with a caption starting with 2—see Figure 8.15). For example, crawling the site socscibot.wlv. ac.uk, then entering the URL socscibot.wlv.ac.uk/help/ in the second yellow text box, ensures that only pages with URLs containing socscibot.wlv.ac.uk/help/ will be included in the crawl.

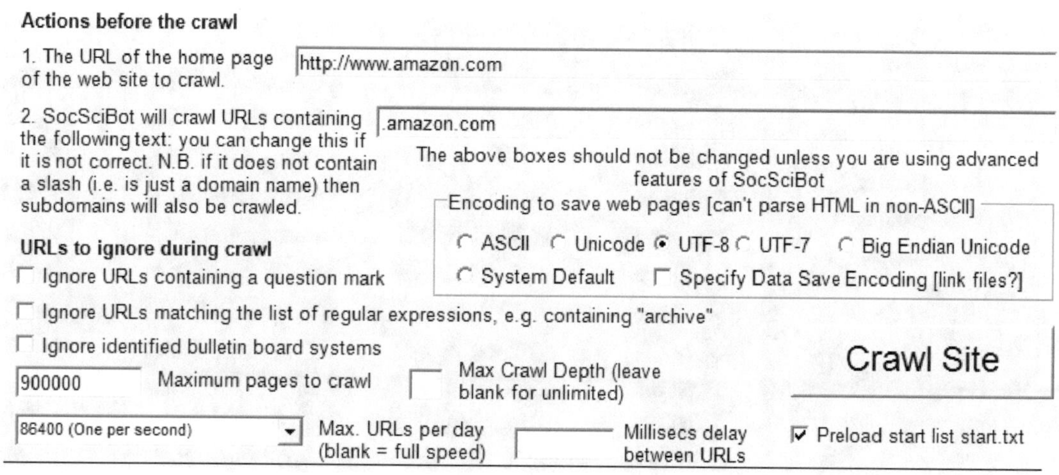

Actions before the crawl

1. The URL of the home page of the web site to crawl.

`http://www.amazon.com`

2. SocSciBot will crawl URLs containing the following text: you can change this if it is not correct. N.B. if it does not contain a slash (i.e. is just a domain name) then subdomains will also be crawled.

`.amazon.com`

The above boxes should not be changed unless you are using advanced features of SocSciBot

URLs to ignore during crawl

☐ Ignore URLs containing a question mark

Encoding to save web pages [can't parse HTML in non-ASCII]

○ ASCII   ○ Unicode   ⦿ UTF-8   ○ UTF-7   ○ Big Endian Unicode
○ System Default   ☐ Specify Data Save Encoding [link files?]

☐ Ignore URLs matching the list of regular expressions, e.g. containing "archive"

☐ Ignore identified bulletin board systems

`900000`   Maximum pages to crawl

☐ Max Crawl Depth (leave blank for unlimited)

Crawl Site

`86400 (One per second)` ▼   Max. URLs per day (blank = full speed)   ☐ Millisecs delay between URLs   ☑ Preload start list start.txt

Figure 8.15: A section of the main SocSciBot interface, showing the main Crawl Site button, the URL of the start page (top right), the site specification text (second from top, right). The option to preload a list of URLs to crawl has been checked (bottom right).

8.17.2 PARSING THE CRAWLED TEXT

Once a crawl is complete, the appropriate Webometric Analyst parsing option for the site can be used to extract data from the crawled pages. When Webometric Analyst requests a folder of crawled webpages, the root folder of the SocSciBot crawl should be selected (i.e., www.wlv.ac.uk in Figure 8.16). The result of the processing is always a tab-delimited plain text file that can be loaded into a spreadsheet for analysis. Normally, each webpage is converted to a single row in the spreadsheet. At the time of writing, Webometric Analyst included functions for extracting information from crawls of Academia.edu, ResearchGate, Google Code, Google Patents, FigShare, SlideShare, some news websites and ClinicalTrials.gov.

Name	Date modified	Type	Size
0.htm	23/04/2016 16:49	Chrome HTML Do...	2 KB
1.htm	23/04/2016 16:49	Chrome HTML Do...	263 KB
2.htm	23/04/2016 16:50	Chrome HTML Do...	256 KB
3.htm	23/04/2016 16:50	Chrome HTML Do...	255 KB
4.htm	23/04/2016 16:50	Chrome HTML Do...	255 KB
5.htm	23/04/2016 16:50	Chrome HTML Do...	263 KB
6.htm	23/04/2016 16:50	Chrome HTML Do...	255 KB
7.htm	23/04/2016 16:50	Chrome HTML Do...	262 KB
8.htm	23/04/2016 16:50	Chrome HTML Do...	264 KB
9.htm	23/04/2016 16:50	Chrome HTML Do...	255 KB
10 htm	23/04/2016 16:50	Chrome HTML Do	263 KB

Figure 8.16: The folder structure created by SocSciBot for a web crawl. The folder *crawler_data* contains all projects. The project folder above is called *A test project*. The pages crawled from the website www.wlv.ac.uk are contained within numerous sub-subfolders of the subfolder *www.wlv.ac.uk*. Each crawled webpage is saved with a numerical filename, such as *5.htm*. When parsing the above crawl with Webometric Analyst, the folder *www.wlv.ac.uk* should be selected and then Webometric Analyst will automatically find all webpages in all sub-subfolders.

8.17.3 CLINICALTRIALS.GOV

This section illustrates the crawling/extraction process with a specific example. The ClinicalTrials.gov website contains a record of all current clinical trials in the U.S. and many from the rest of the world. The site is designed to encourage crawling so that the information in it can be analysed. As part of this it has (at the time of writing) a copy of the site designed for crawlers at https://www.clinicaltrials.gov/ct2/crawl/. To crawl this site, this URL can be entered as the starting page for a SocSciBot crawl.

Once the crawl is finished (over 200,000 pages, taking several days) all of the crawler-friendly pages will be saved to the local computer. These saved files can then be processed with Webometric Analyst's menu option for this site, which is the ClinicalTrials.gov options in the Services menu (there is a second option for processing citations in the Citations menu). The output of Webometric Analyst's parsing of SocSciBot's crawl of ClinicalTrials.gov is a set of tab-delimited plain text files with different types of information. These files can be loaded into a spreadsheet to read. For example, one of the files contains a summary of how often MESH keywords appear in the crawled pages (Figure 8.17).

MeshTerm	Frequency
Pharmacologic Actions	83896
Therapeutic Uses	67085
Physiological Effects of Drugs	54333
Neoplasms	40793
Antineoplastic Agents	26024

Figure 8.17: A list of frequencies of MESH keywords from ClinicalTrials.gov pages crawled by SocS-ciBot, extracted by Webometric Analyst and loaded into a spreadsheet.

8.18   SUMMARY

Raw indicator data can be automatically collected for sets of documents in various ways using Webometric Analyst, SocSciBot and Mozdeh. When collecting new data, it is good practice to run a small-scale pilot test first and to look at the data collected afterwards to check that it makes sense and that there has not been a problem with the data collection process. The simplest collection process is for Mendeley readers, since this converts a file of publication information by adding Mendeley reader counts in one single step. The other methods involve several different automated strategies: constructing and submitting Bing queries; crawling a site and extracting information from the downloaded pages; or a multiple stage process to download and filter the results. In all cases it is also possible to gather the data manually for a few documents, and thus the purpose of using the software is to gather the same information efficiently for a large set of documents. The following chapters give information about indicator formulae that can be useful for comparing the average impact of sets of documents against each other or the world average.

CHAPTER 9

Indicator Formulae and Experimental Considerations

This chapter describes formulae for processing web indicators as well as issues that are important for researchers designing studies to investigate or exploit web indicators. Some of these issues are primarily statistical, such as the choice of correlation test and appropriate modelling approaches, but others involve details about the way in which citations accrue, such as the need for citation windows and the importance of disciplinary differences. This chapter is mainly theoretical but the following chapter describes how to calculate many of the indictors with Webometric Analyst.

Many techniques described below give confidence intervals for indicator values for sets of scholarly outputs. These confidence intervals must be interpreted with caution for two reasons. First, all data sets are likely to violate the statistical independence assumption needed for the confidence intervals to be fully valid. Second, all web indicator data can be flawed and so if one group has statistically significantly higher values on an educational indicator than another then it is far from certain that the first has had more educational impact. This is because the higher values may be due to the flaws in the indicator data—such as more publicity-related content or a higher online profile for one group—rather than genuinely higher educational impact. Thus, the limitations of the indicator data and the context of the application (see Chapter 7) should not be forgotten when applying statistical techniques.

9.1 BASIC INDICATOR FORMULAE

It is common to process indicator data with a standard mathematical formula in order to produce an informative statistic. The use of formulae makes it possible to compare between groups of outputs rather than just between individual publications. The following are straightforward methods for estimating the average of a set of indicator values. They are only appropriate for sets of outputs from the same field and year.

- **Arithmetic mean:** The simplest way to compare indicator data between two sets of outputs is to compare the average score between them. The arithmetic mean is appropriate for this except when the data set is highly skewed. Since most indicator data is highly skewed, with many low values and few high values, the arithmetic mean is rarely a good choice. For raw data $\{x_i\}$ the arithmetic mean formula is: $\bar{x} = \frac{1}{n} \Sigma x_i$.

- **Median:** The median is the middle value (of the average of the two middle values) when a set of numbers is ordered from smallest to largest. It is a more reliable measure of average for skewed data than is the arithmetic mean but it is not useful if the data are typically numbers close to zero because it is not discriminating enough. For example, in most academic fields and years, the median citation count would be under 5 so there is not much scope to distinguish between the medians of groups of articles. The median is useful when the data values tend to be large, such as for usage indicators, but is useless when most values are zero, as for many web indicators.

- **Geometric mean:** This is a formula for the average that is more appropriate than the arithmetic mean for skewed data and is more discriminatory than the median when the data values tend to be small. Hence it should be the default measure of average for indicator data, except in the case of usage data, where the median is equally appropriate. Since academic indicator data typically contain many zeros and the standard geometric mean cannot be calculated if any of the data values are zero, an offset of 1 should be used in its calculation. If the raw data is $\{x_i\}$ then the offset geometric mean formula is $\check{x} = \exp(\frac{1}{n} \sum \ln(1+x_i)) - 1$. This is discussed in more detail in Section 9.5.

9.2 CITATION WINDOWS AND THE INFLUENCE OF TIME ON INDICATORS

Citation counts and most web indicators accrue over time, starting at zero before an output has been published in any form, and perhaps eventually reaching a final value, after which the output is effectively forgotten, obsolete or incorporated within the newer literature. It is not fair to directly compare the indicator values of newer outputs with those of older outputs because the older outputs have had more time to attract attention. This is a problem if analysing outputs that have been published at different points in time.

Scopus and WoS citations to books and articles are relatively slow to accumulate, often taking several years to build up a substantial fraction of the eventual citation count. This is because other scholars need time after a paper has been published to read it, incorporate it into their own research, conduct that research and then get the research published. The publication lifecycle alone can easily add a year of delays because of refereeing and also the need for revisions and additional rounds of refereeing. In contrast, as soon as an article is published it may be tweeted about. Because Twitter is often seen as a real-time medium, articles may attract a substantial fraction of their eventual number of tweets within a few weeks of publication. In between these two, Mendeley probably mirrors citation counts except for the publication delays and so accumulates values about a year earlier than for citations. Mendeley also has the additional property that readers may disappear from an article if they delete their Mendeley profile or prune their publication lists as their interests evolve. Thus, Mendeley reader counts may decrease a small amount over time. Syllabus mentions probably also decrease substantially in the long run as old syllabi are pruned from the web (Figure 9.1). All web indicators probably fall somewhere between the extremes shown in Figure 9.1.

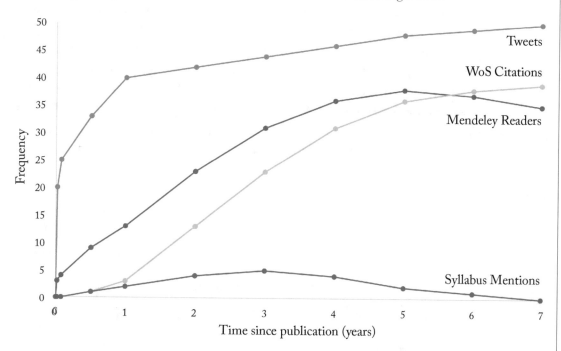

Figure 9.1: A graph using artificial data to illustrate possible changes over time in the number of tweets, citations, readers and syllabus mentions for an article. Tweets appear the most rapidly, including within the first week of publication, whereas citations and syllabus mentions are the slowest to accumulate. Syllabus mentions can be expected to eventually disappear and Mendeley readers may decline slightly in the long run as readers leave or prune their Mendeley libraries.

There are two traditional solutions to the problem of time differences for citation counts. The first is to use a citation window. With this policy, citations to articles are only counted if they appear within a fixed number of years of the publication of the article, such as three years. Thus, for an article published in 2013, its citations to 2016 would be counted, whereas for an article published in 2012, its articles to 2015 would be counted. This is a reasonable solution but imperfect because citation databases change in size over time (normally increasing—see Figure 9.2) and so an article published in 2000 could expect fewer Scopus or WoS citations in the three years after publication than an article published in 2010. The same has been true for many web indicators as the web and social websites have increased in size. A practical problem with this solution for indicators is that it is usually impossible or difficult to separate out the mentions or citations from a particular set of years. For example, the Mendeley website and API report the total number of readers of an article but not when the article was registered by these readers. Similarly, while all tweets are date stamped and so it would be possible to count Twitter citations from any desired date range, some altmetric data sources might just report the overall total number of tweet citations and not the individual tweets. A better solution is only to compare articles with other articles published in the same year. Although this is still unfair on articles published later in the year that have had less time to accumulate indicator scores, especially when the year is relatively recent, this seems like a practical compromise. For very recent articles, if it is possible to time slice by half a year or month, then this would help to reduce the effect of time. If it is essential to compare articles from multiple different years, then field- and year-normalised indicators can be calculated that calculate separately by year but then combine articles from different years in a relatively fair way (see Section 9.6).

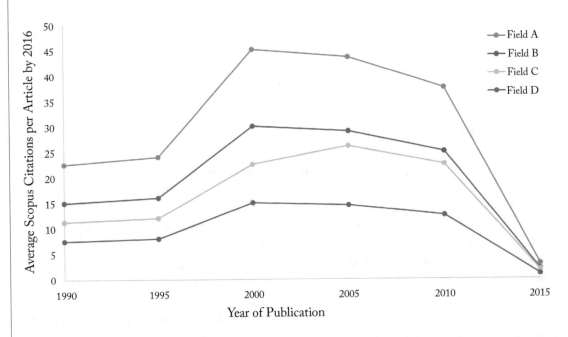

Figure 9.2: An illustration of the effect of citation database changes over time (artificial data). Older articles tend to be more highly cited than more recent articles and this is true from 2005 onwards. There was a large database expansion some time between 1995 and 2000, resulting in higher citation counts for articles from 2000 than for articles from 1995. There was also a small database expansion in field C between 2000 and 2005, resulting in a second average citation count increase for articles from 2005.

9.3   DISCIPLINARY AND TIME DIFFERENCES

Academic disciplines have greatly different goals, cultures and working practices (Becher and Trowler, 2001; Hyland, 2004; Whitley, 2000). These differences extend to citation practices in terms of what is cited, how often typical outputs are cited and why citations are used. This lack of uniformity is likely to apply to all web indicators as well.

Articles from different fields can attract citations and web attention at greatly different rates (Figures 9.3, 9.4). The average number of citations per article in some areas of medicine can be many times as high as the average number of citations per article in most areas of the arts and humanities, for example. It is unfair to directly compare the indicator values of sets of articles with each other if they are from different disciplines or contain different mixes of articles from different disciplines.

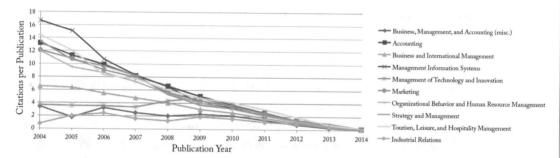

Figure 9.3: This graph of citations per publication over time shows that the average number of citations per paper can vary greatly even between similar subfields of a major field. In this case, the average number of citations per paper for older articles in Management Information Systems is an order of magnitude larger than for Industrial Relations (Figure 8 of Thelwall and Sud, in press).

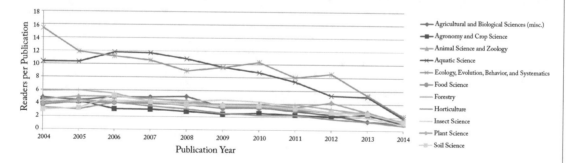

Figure 9.4: This graph of Mendeley readers per paper over time shows that the average number of Mendeley readers per paper can vary greatly even between similar subfields of a major field. In this case, within Agricultural and Biological Sciences the average number of readers per paper for older articles in Ecology is four times larger than for Soil Science (Figure 13 of Thelwall and Sud, in press).

The simplest solution to the issue of disciplinary differences is to only compare articles against others from the same field. This assumes that it is possible to categorise the articles by field. The subject categories of Scopus and WoS can be used for this although they are imperfect and within these categories there can be higher and lower citation areas. Using these categories will at least reduce the problem of citation differences. If it is essential to compare articles from multiple disciplines with each other, then a field- and year-normalised indicator can be used that calculates separately by field first and then combines the fields in an unbiased way (see Section 9.6). This solution is difficult to apply to other types of research outputs, including books and non-standard outputs, because these are often not found within any suitable academic field-based classification scheme. Thus, for these types of resource the only current practical solution is to use an ad-hoc classification—and even a very broad one will help—or to proceed without field classification but report caveats about the unreliability of the results.

9.4   CORRELATION TESTS

As discussed in Section 2.1.2, correlation tests are important methods for evaluating new web indicators. Citation data and most types of alternative indicator data are highly skewed (Figures 9.5 and 9.6). They have many low values—zero is often the most common number—and a few high values. Because of this, the Pearson correlation test cannot be used to compare them with each other or with other data sources for evaluations (see Section 2.1.2). The Pearson correlation coefficient is inappropriate because the statistical probabilities associated with the test assume that the two correlated samples are drawn from normally distributed populations. The simplest way around this problem is to use the Spearman correlation instead. This assesses only the rank orders when calculating correlations and so it does not matter if the data is skewed.

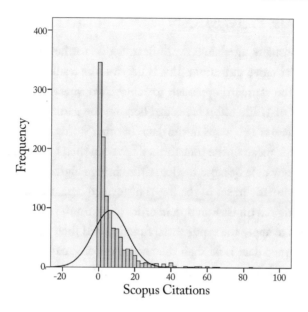

Figure 9.5: The skewed distribution of Scopus citations for orthodontics articles from 2009. There are many low values and a small number of very high values. A normal distribution curve is superimposed.

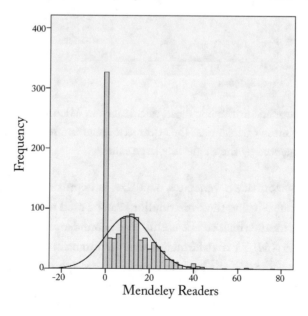

Figure 9.6: The skewed distribution of Mendeley readers for Orthodontics articles from 2009. There are many low values and a small number of high values. A normal distribution curve is superimposed.

9.5   THE GEOMETRIC MEAN

The arithmetic mean is usually unreliable for indicators due to the highly skewed nature of citation counts and most alternative indicators. This is because the results can be greatly influenced by individual high values. The standard approach to remove skewness is to use a logarithmic transformation with an offset of 1. The offset is needed because the natural logarithm of 0 is undefined. Adding 1 ensures that there are no zeros in the data. In other words, each citation count is replaced by $ln(1 + c)$. The arithmetic mean of the transformed data can then be taken and this will be less affected by outliers in the raw data because the logarithm brings high numbers much closer together. After calculating the arithmetic mean of the log-transformed data, the answer can be transformed with the reverse of the original transformation in order to return the mean to the original scale. This reverse transformation is to apply the exponential function and then subtract 1. So if the arithmetic mean of the log-transformed data is M then the reverse transformation gives $exp(M) - 1$. The final result is known as the geometric mean (see Figure 9.7 for an example). This has been applied to Mendeley readers as well as citations (Fairclough and Thelwall, 2015).

	A	B	C	D
1	**Article**	**Citations**	**Log(1+citations)**	**Formula used**
2	A	0	0.000	=LN(1+C2)
3	B	1	0.693	=LN(1+C3)
4	C	2	1.099	=LN(1+C4)
5	D	5	1.792	=LN(1+C5)
6	E	100	4.615	=LN(1+C6)
7	Arithmetic mean	21.6	1.640	=AVERAGE(C2:C6)
8	Geometric mean		4.154	=EXP(C7)-1

Figure 9.7: Geometric mean and arithmetic mean calculations in Microsoft Excel, showing the formulae used for all geometric mean calculations. The arithmetic mean is not a good measure of the average here because it is too influenced by the single very large value.

If the $ln(1+c)$ transformation generates data that is approximately normal, then standard normal distribution formulae (using the t-distribution) can be used to calculate 95% confidence intervals for the geometric mean, which can be useful. These confidence intervals should be calculated before making the final $exp(M) - 1$ transformation and then transformed with the same formula. It would be reasonable to assume that the log transformed data is approximately normally distributed in most cases because several studies have shown citation (Thelwall, 2016c) and some alternative indicator data (Thelwall and Wilson, 2016) to follow the lognormal distribution quite closely, and a log transformation of this generates the normal distribution.

The geometric mean should only be calculated for collections of outputs from a single field and year, if possible. When this is not possible, a caveat about field and year differences should accompany the results. If data is available for multiple fields and/or years, then the geometric mean can be calculated separately for each one. Field- and year-normalised indicators (discussed below) can be used instead if a single number is needed for a set of articles from multiple fields or years. For a set of n articles with citation or alternative indicator values $c_1, c_2, \ldots c_n$ the geometric mean is $\exp\left(\frac{\ln(1 + c_1) + \ln(1 + c_2) + \ldots \ln(1 + c_n)}{n}\right) - 1$.

9.6   MNLCS: FIELD- AND YEAR-NORMALISED INDICATORS

Sometimes a single indicator is needed for a set of outputs from multiple fields and/or years. For example, the purpose of an investigation might be to compare UK-authored research to the world average. Although it would be possible to compare the average separately for each field and year, this would generate too many numbers to easily understand and so a common solution is to combine all the numbers through the use of a field-normalised indicator, reporting a separate one for each year. In this way, the comparison is fair, and trends over time can be seen (e.g., Elsevier, 2013). This method can also be used for multiple years in order to give a single number for all fields and years combined.

Essentially, the approach for field-normalised indicators that use a measure of average citation counts (or other indicator scores) is to calculate the world average (geometric mean or arithmetic mean) separately for each field and year and then divide the raw citation counts (or indicator scores) by the world average for their field and year. These normalised indicator values then have a world average of 1 (at least if the arithmetic mean is used—the average is close to 1 if the geometric mean is used). If the average of these normalised values for a subgroup is above 1 then its publications tend to be above the world average and if it is below 1 then it is below the world average. There are three main variations of this that are relatively straightforward to calculate with indicator data. More complex variants that may give more fine-grained field normalisation (e.g., Bornmann and Haunschild, 2016) are not covered here.

- **Mean-normalised Citation Score (MNCS):** For each field and year, the data is divided by the arithmetic mean of all the world's articles from that field and year (Waltman et al., 2011). The arithmetic mean of the normalised values for each field and year is then taken. This is not ideal for highly skewed data sets because of the use of the arithmetic mean. For a set of n articles with citation or alternative indicator values $c_1, c_2, \ldots c_n$ and with a_i being the arithmetic mean of the world's papers from the same field and year as c_i the MNCS is $(c_1/a_1 + c_2/a_2 + \cdots c_n/a_n)/n$.

- **Geometric Mean-normalised Citation Score (gMNCS):** For each field and year, the data is divided by the geometric mean of all the world's articles from that field and year (Thelwall and Sud, 2016). The geometric mean of the normalised values for each field and year is then taken. This is suitable for highly skewed data sets but has the disadvantage that the overall world gMNCS can be slightly different from 1 due to the way in which the geometric mean is calculated. For a set of n articles with citation or alternative indicator values $c_1, c_2, \ldots c_n$ and with g_i being the geometric mean of the world's papers from the same field and year as c_1 the gMNCS is $\exp((\ln(1 + c_1/g_i) + \ln(1 + c_2/g_2) + \ln(1 + c_n/g_n))/n) - 1$.

- **Mean Normalised Log-transformed Citation Score (MNLCS):** This is the same as the MNCS except that before any calculations start, the data are normalised by adding 1 and then taking their natural logarithm (Thelwall, submitted). This transformation greatly reduces or eliminates the skewness of the data and makes this method appropriate for skewed indicator data. This is preferable to the gMNCS for ease of interpretation because the world MNLCS score is always exactly 1. For a set of n articles with citation or alternative indicator values $c_1, c_2, \ldots c_n$ and with l_i being the arithmetic mean of the $ln(1 + c)$ log transformed world's papers from the same field and year as c_i, the MNLCS is $(\ln(1 + c_1)/l_1 + \ln(1 + c_2)/l_2 + \cdots \ln(1 + c_n)/l_n)/n$.

Confidence limits can be calculated for MNLCS values using Fieller's (1954) method, which is implemented in Webometric Analyst.

Table 9.1 Illustrates the calculations necessary for the above indicators to be applied to the Tweets to a set of five articles from two different fields and years. The "world" means have been calculated separately from a complete collection of articles in each field. The three indicator values are in the bottom row of the table.

- For the MNCS, the Tweets column in Table 9.1 is divided by the world arithmetic mean column to give the MNCS value column. The arithmetic mean of the MNCS value column is then the final MNCS.

- For the gMNCS, the Tweets column is divided by the world geometric mean column to give the gMNCS value column. The geometric mean of the gMNCS value column is then the final gMNCS.

- For the MNLCS, the Tweets column is used to calculate the ln(1+ Tweets) column. This is then divided by the world mean of ln(1+ Tweets) column to give the MNLCS value column. The arithmetic mean of the MNLCS value column is then the final MNLCS.

Table 9.1: Calculations for the MNCS (1.9), gMNCS (2.207) and MNLCS (1.876) for a set of 5 articles. The bottom row contains the arithmetic mean for the MNCS and MNLCS but the geometric mean for the gMNCS.

Article	Tweets	ln(1 + Tweets)	Field	Year	World Arithmetic Mean	World Geographic Mean	World Mean of ln(1+ Tweets)	MNCS Value	gMNCS Value	MLNCS Value
1	10	2.398	A	2015	5	4	1	2	2.5	2.398
2	30	3.434	A	2015	5	4	1	6	7.5	3.434
3	5	1.792	B	2015	4	3	0.7	1.25	1.667	2.560
4	1	0.693	B	2015	4	3	0.7	0.25	0.333	0.990
5	0	0	B	2016	2	1	0.5	0	0	0
Mean								**1.9**	**2.207**	**1.876**

The formulae above assume that each article fits within a single subject category. If an article is assigned to multiple subject categories then its contribution to the formula for each individual subject category should be multiplied by 1/n where n is the number of subject categories that the article is assigned to (following: Waltman et al., 2011). Thus, the article is essentially shared equally between the subject categories. This balances out the difference between the citation rates of the categories in which the article is placed.

An alternative method to create an indicator that is not influenced by the skewness of the dataset is to calculate the percentage of articles within the top X% (see Section 9.7). This has the advantage of being more transparent than the mean but the disadvantages of producing multiple indicators and being less precise (Thelwall, 2016b).

In order to calculate field-normalised indicators, a complete set of indicator values is needed for all the world's publications in each field and year for which there is an article in the data set to be evaluated. In practice, all publications from relevant Scopus or WoS categories are usually used instead. In situations when indicator data is slow or expensive to collect, an alternative is to take a random sample of, say, 500 of the world's publications for each field and year in order to cut down the total amount of indicator data to be collected. As long as the sample is random and large enough, then this should not affect the results much.

9.7   PROPORTION OF NON-ZERO VALUES

For data which is essentially binary in the sense that all or almost all values are either 0 or 1, the most relevant statistic for a set of papers is the proportion that have non-zero values. This also needs to be used for web indicators when nearly all publications have a zero value and confidence limits are needed because these tend to be very wide or undefined for the MNLCS. To illustrate this, suppose that the publications of two departments are being compared using a patent citation indicator.

- Department A has published 100 papers and 10 of them have received one patent citation, so 10% of Department A's papers have received patent citations and Department A's papers have received an average of 0.1 patent citations each.

- Department B has published 200 papers with 14 receiving 1 patent citation and 1 receiving 2 patent citations, so 7.5% of Department B's papers have received patent citations and Department B's papers have received an average of 0.08 patent citations each.

On the basis of the above, Department A has a higher proportion of papers with patent citations and a higher average number of patent citations per paper. But it is useful to judge whether differences like this are statistically significant. Department A's data is binary and Department B's data is nearly binary but both are, in theory, drawn from highly skewed distributions (e.g., discrete lognormal) and so the geometric mean is more appropriate than the arithmetic mean and confidence intervals can be calculated for this.

Considering the *proportion* of non-zero indicator values, it is possible to use a difference between proportions test, chi-squared test or confidence interval to assess differences between the proportions for the two departments. This is of interest as an intrinsically valid property of a set of articles and also on the basis that individual indicator scores that are higher than 1 may be due to copying. In the case of patent citations, sometimes there are many patents with almost identical text, including citations, but with minor changes in the invention. This copying can produce high patent citation counts for articles in the reference lists. Alternatively, if there is just one high value then this may be a fluke that is unlikely to be replicated often and so it should not be given a high influence on any calculation. The two different approaches (geometric mean and difference between proportions) seem to give very similar results in practice if the data is mainly binary and so there is no statistical power reason for preferring one over the other.

Wilson's score interval (Wilson, 1927) can be used to calculate confidence intervals for the proportion of non-zero indicator values. For a 95% confidence interval, this gives the following, where $\hat{p}$ is the proportion of articles with a non-zero value (i.e., the sample proportion) and n is the number of articles (i.e., the sample size):

$$\frac{1}{1+\frac{1}{n}1.96^2}\left[\hat{p}+\frac{1}{2n}1.96^2 \pm 1.96\sqrt{\frac{1}{n}\hat{p}(1-\hat{p})+\frac{1}{4n^2}1.96^2}\right]$$

9.7.1   FIELD- AND YEAR-EQUALISED PROPORTIONS

If a data set consists of multiple fields and/or years, then it would be wrong to simply combine all of these together into a single group for a difference in proportions test if the sample sizes differ between fields and/or years. If the proportions differ between fields and years, then this gives an advantage to entities (e.g., departments, countries, research funders) that have published many articles in fields and years with high proportions of non-zero values. In the case of patents, for example, sets of articles with a high percentage of older articles or biochemical engineering articles would have an unfair advantage if all articles were pooled together before calculating the overall proportion of non-zero values.

A solution to the problem of varying percentages is to artificially inflate or deflate the sample sizes to the overall average sample size to ensure that each field and/or year is equally represented. Changing the sample sizes to be equal for each field/year set ensures that no field/year has more influence than any other so that a group has no advantage from publishing more articles in a field/ year with higher world average data values. Setting the sample sizes to be equal to the average also ensures that when the new artificial samples are pooled then the overall sample size is correct so that statistical analyses of the resulting artificial pooled sample should be approximately correct. If a sample size is zero in any field/year set, then it should be removed from the calculation because bias correction would not be possible for it.

In the example below (Table 9.2), Group A is to be compared against Group B and the world average using data from three fields. If no bias correction is used then Group A would have an unfair overall advantage because it published more articles (500) than did Group B (400) in Field 2, which has the highest world proportion of non-zero indicator values (0.06). If the raw data is replaced with the adjusted data (i.e., the adjusted rows in the table) then each field is equally represented for both groups and so the comparison of the pooled samples would be unbiased. From these figures, it can be seen that the tendency is for more of B's articles (0.2222) to have non-zero scores in comparison to A's articles (0.2167). A statistical test or confidence intervals could be used to assess the statistical significance of the difference.

Table 9.2: Calculations to adjust sample sizes to ensure unbiased comparisons of overall proportions of articles with non-zero indicator values between data sets. The adjusted data sets have equal sample sizes that are the mean of the sample sizes for the individual fields.

Data set	Statistic	Field 1	Field 2	Field 3	Mean	Pooled	Comment
World	Total articles	10000	5000	6000	7000	21000	Biased
World	Non zero	400	300	800		1500	Biased
World	Proportion	0.04	0.06	0.1333		0.0714	Biased
Adj. world	Total articles	7000	7000	7000		21000	Unbiased
Adj. world	Non zero	280	420	933.3		1633.3	Unbiased

Data set	Statistic	Field 1	Field 2	Field 3	Mean	Pooled	Comment
Adj. world	Proportion	0.04	0.06	0.1333		0.0778	Unbiased
Group A	Total articles	500	500	200	400	1200	Biased
Group A	Non zero	100	100	50		250	Biased
Group A	Proportion	0.2	0.2	0.25		0.2083	Biased
Adjusted A	Total articles	400	400	400		1200	Unbiased
Adjusted A	Non zero	80	80	100		260	Unbiased
Adjusted A	Proportion	0.2	0.2	0.25		0.2167	Unbiased
Group B	Total articles	900	400	200	500	1500	Biased
Group B	Non zero	150	100	50		300	Biased
Group B	Proportion	0.1667	0.25	0.25		0.2000	Biased
Adjusted B	Total articles	500	500	500		1500	Unbiased
Adjusted B	Non zero	83.3	125	125		333.3	Unbiased
Adjusted B	Proportion	0.1667	0.25	0.25		0.2222	Unbiased

9.8   NPC: NORMALISED PROPORTION CITED

The equalised proportion cited can be normalised by dividing it by the world average equalised proportion cited for the same fields. In mathematical notation, the world-normalised proportion cited (NPC) for each group g compared to the world w is the ratio of the field- and year-equalised sample proportions (Thelwall, submitted).

$$NPC = \hat{p}_g/\hat{p}_w$$

Now $\hat{p}_g/\hat{p}_w > 1$ implies that g has a greater proportion of cited articles than the world average for the fields that it publishes in. This mirrors the situation for the MNLCS. The ratio of two proportions is a risk ratio, and there are standard techniques for calculating lower NPC_L and upper NPC_U confidence limits for such ratios (Bailey, 1987). If a data set has a high proportion of zeros then these limits are likely to be narrower than the MNLCS limits (Thelwall, submitted), and so NPC is preferred in this case.

$$NPC_L = \exp\left(\ln\left(\frac{\hat{p}_g}{\hat{p}_w}\right) - 1.96\sqrt{\frac{(n_g - \hat{p}_g n_g)/\hat{p}_g n_g}{n_g} + \frac{(n_w - \hat{p}_w n_w)/\hat{p}_w n_w}{n_w}}\right)$$

$$NPC_U = \exp\left(\ln\left(\frac{\hat{p}_g}{\hat{p}_w}\right) + 1.96\sqrt{\frac{(n_g - \hat{p}_g n_g)/\hat{p}_g n_g}{n_g} + \frac{(n_w - \hat{p}_w n_w)/\hat{p}_w n_w}{n_w}}\right)$$

Here, n_g and n_w are the combined group and world sample sizes, respectively, so that $\hat{p}_g n_g$ and $\hat{p}_w n_w$ in the formula are the numbers of group and world articles cited. A continuity correction (adding 0.5 to the number of cited articles for both the group and the world classes for the confidence interval width calculations) should be included in case the number of uncited articles is very small. The confidence limits are unreliable if some field/year combinations have much fewer articles than others, so if this is the case then the small field/year combinations should be removed first. These calculations are available through the Webometric Analyst *Reports* menu.

9.9   REGRESSION ANALYSES

Statistical regression techniques can be useful to give evidence of the factors that influence an indicator. For example, a regression analysis might reveal that articles by authors from some countries tend to generate higher indicator values than authors from other countries. The simplest regression technique is ordinary least squares regression. This is inappropriate, however, because it requires that the residuals are approximately normally distributed whereas most indicator data sets are highly skewed.

A solution to the skewed data problem is to use a logarithmic transformation to reduce or eliminate the amount of skewness. For citation counts, the transformation $ln(1 + c)$ is effective at this. In other words, add 1 to all citation counts and then take the natural log of the result. After this the data is likely to be close enough to being normally distributed for ordinary least squares linear regression to work (Thelwall, 2016a). This solution is also recommended for web indicators because they can have the same problem of highly skewed data.

9.10   COMPARING RECENTLY PUBLISHED ARTICLES: THE SIGN TEST

Correlations between alternative indicators and citation counts can be misleading even for articles from a single field and year. The reason is that the use of the social web is rapidly increasing and so recent articles may have more mentions on the social web (and particularly on microblogs), on average, than older articles whereas older articles are likely to have more citations than newer ones, and so there is a bias towards negative correlations between social web indicators and citation counts. The standard method to minimise time biases in scientometrics is to use a short citation window (e.g., one year) for a significant period in the past (e.g., at least 3–5 years ago) to minimise the effect of the time differences. The use of such a citation window is a disadvantage for social web indicators because of the possible changes in average values during a single year. In response to this issue, a new test has been developed, the sign test (Thelwall et al., 2013a).

The sign test is a simple method to avoid biases caused by time differences. Suppose that three articles are published consecutively and that after a period of time they have attracted c_1, c_2 and c_3 citations and s_1, s_2 and s_3 scores on a particular web indicator. The sign test assesses whether a prediction of the difference in citations for the middle article compared to the others would be successful, based upon any difference in altmetric score for the middle article compared to the altmetric scores of the others. The test has three possible outcomes.

- Success: $s_2 > (s_1 + s_3)/2$ and $c_2 > (c_1 + c_3)/2$

- Success: $s_2 < (s_1 + s_3)/2$ and $c_2 < (c_1 + c_3)/2$

- Fail: $s_2 > (s_1 + s_3)/2$ and $c_2 < (c_1 + c_3)/2$

- Fail: : $s_2 < (s_1 + s_3)/2$ and $c_2 > (c_1 + c_3)/2$

- Null: All other cases.

In other words, s_2 must be different from the average of s_1 and s_3 to get a result other than null. If s_2 is larger than the average of s_1 and s_3, then the alternative indicator predicts that the citations, c_2 for the middle article should also be larger than the average citations for the other two articles, $(c_1+c_3)/2$. If this is true, the test is a success. If it is false then the test is a fail, unless the scores are equal, in which case the result is null. The logic reverses if s_2 is smaller than the average of s_1 and s_3. The sign test is to compare the number of successes with the number of failures for this test over a large number of articles. If the number of successes is significantly higher than the number of failures, then this gives evidence that if time were eliminated then citation counts and altmetric scores would correlate. The limitations of the sign test include all the limitations of the correlation test except for time bias and include an extra limitation that the size of the sign test proportion is not a reliable indicator of the strength of any underlying relationship. Hence, in statistical terms the sign test cannot be used for evidence of the effect size (in terms of the correlation magnitude) of the prediction.

The sign test can, in theory, be modified to make predictions based upon additional adjacent articles in the following logical way, where $n > 1$ can be any whole number. Using a larger n makes the test more stable due to the greater degree of averaging, but reduces the total number of articles that can be tested.

- Success: $s_i > (\sum_{\substack{j=i-n \\ j \neq i}}^{i+n} s_j)/2n$ and $c_i > (\sum_{\substack{j=i-n \\ j \neq i}}^{i+n} c_j)/2n$

- Success: $s_i < (\sum_{\substack{j=i-n \\ j \neq i}}^{i+n} s_j)/2n$ and $c_i < (\sum_{\substack{j=i-n \\ j \neq i}}^{i+n} c_j)/2n$

- Fail: $s_i > (\sum_{\substack{j=i-n \\ j \neq i}}^{i+n} s_j)/2n$ and $c_i < (\sum_{\substack{j=i-n \\ j \neq i}}^{i+n} c_j)/2n$

- Fail: $s_i < (\sum_{\substack{j=i-n \\ j \neq i}}^{i+n} s_j)/2n$ and $c_i > (\sum_{\substack{j=i-n \\ j \neq i}}^{i+n} c_j)/2n$

- Null: All other cases.

9.11 SUMMARY

The indicator formulae introduced in this chapter are designed to give powerful and fair techniques to compare or evaluate the impact of collections of documents with any of the web indicators, or with citation counts. The most important decision to make is whether to use MNLCS or NPC, with the latter being preferred for web indicators when most of the raw data values are 0. Thus, comparing the proportion of outputs with a non-zero score can be useful even if the average scores for the sets of outputs compared are low. The formulae include confidence intervals so that the statistical significance of the difference between two values can be assessed. The formulae and confidence intervals are all built into Webometric Analyst in order to simplify the process of calculating them.

CHAPTER 10

Calculating Indicators with Webometric Analyst

This chapter describes the functions available in Webometric Analyst to calculate field- and/or year-normalised indicators from a web indicator data set. These allow fair comparisons between sets of outputs. Field- and year-normalised indicators are a basic requirement for research evaluations, as argued above (Section 9.3), and are routinely used for citation counts.

It was difficult in the past to calculate field normalised-values for books because they had not been systematically categorised into fields. Today, both the Web of Science Book Citation Index and Scopus include tens of thousands of books categorised by subject, and so this problem has reduced. Nevertheless, the proportion of the world's recent academic books that have been categorised by these two sources is probably very small (e.g., Torres-Salinas et al., 2014) and so any evaluation of a set of books is likely to find that the majority need to be manually categorised first. In addition, the coverage of these databases seems to be quite selective, but in different ways, and so it is not clear how informative any field-normalised book figure would be based upon samples from them.

10.1 INDICATORS FROM BING SEARCH DATA

A set of standard indicators (e.g., arithmetic mean, geometric mean, field-normalised indicators) can be calculated by Webometric Analyst from the results of its Bing searches for web indicators (e.g., syllabus citations, Wikipedia mentions). There are two procedures, one for just calculating the indicators and one for comparing the indicators for a subset of documents against the corresponding indicators from an entire field using field normalisation. The latter procedure is designed for evaluations in which the average impact of a set of documents (e.g., from a research group, or funded by a particular organisation) is compared against the world average.

10.1.1 SEPARATE INDICATORS FOR EACH SET OF BING SEARCH RESULTS

If indicators are needed from Bing search results, then the original search files must be separated out by field and year so that each set of articles or books from the same field and year is in a different file. This is important because it does not make sense to calculate indicators from collections of articles that mix fields and years (see Section 9.3). Putting articles or books into separate files by field and year in this way is necessary to flag to Webometric Analyst that they need to be processed separately.

To calculate a set of indicators for saved Bing searches, from the *Reports* menu, select the *Calculate MNLCS and gMNCS for a set of web searches (one or more files, each processed separately)* menu option. It will calculate a range of indicators for each file, saving the results to a new plain text file, such as the one in Figure 10.1. This contains the arithmetic and geometric mean as well as the arithmetic mean of the log-normalised data. A 95% confidence interval is also given for some of the indicators.

As can be seen from Figure 10.1, a separate value is calculated for URLs, domains, sites, STLDs and TLDs (see Section 8.5.1 for an explanation of terms). Although all five values are provided for completeness, only one should be used in any evaluation. Normally, the unique domains value is the best option. This counts the number of different web domains that match the Bing query and avoids the problem that a citation may occur multiple times in a single domain due to copying, artificially inflating the URL count. For Wikipedia citations, the URL count may be preferred because Wikipedia does not seem to have extensive copying of citations, although there is some copying between different language versions (Kousha and Thelwall, in press-c).

World file: General Nursing 2010_search_ppt
Queries: 499
Arithmetic mean (unique URLs): 0.080200
Arithmetic mean (unique domains): 0.050100
Arithmetic mean (unique sites): 0.050100
Arithmetic mean (unique STLDs): 0.050100
Arithmetic mean (unique TLDs): 0.050100
Mean (95%CI) of log (1+unique URLs): 0.044323 (0.038388, 0.058242)
Mean (95%CI) of log (1+unique domains): 0.034727 (0.021310, 0.048143)
Mean (95%CI) of log (1+unique sites): 0.034727 (0.021310, 0.048143)
Mean (95%CI) of log (1+unique STLDs): 0.034727 (0.021310, 0.048143)
Mean (95%CI) of log (1+unique TLDs): 0.034727 (0.021310, 0.048143)
Geometric mean (95%CI) of unique URLs: 0.045481 (0.031333, 0.059828)
Geometric mean (95%CI) of unique domains: 0.035337 (0.021539, 0.049321)
Geometric mean (95%CI) of unique sites: 0.035337 (0.021539, 0.049321)
Geometric mean (95%CI) of unique STLDs: 0.035337 (0.021539, 0.049321)
Geometric mean (95%CI) of unique TLDs: 0.035337 (0.021539, 0.049321)
Proportion non-zero (95%CI): 0.06000 (0.02043, 0.17490)

Figure 10.1: An extract from a report summarising a range of indicators for the file General Nursing 2010_search_ppt of Bing search results for PowerPoint searches to General Nursing articles from 2010.

10.1.2   FIELD-NORMALISED INDICATORS TO COMPARE SUBGROUPS TO THE WORLD AVERAGE

It is sometimes useful to compare a subgroup of articles to a larger group or the world average. This subgroup could be the set of all articles created by a single research group or funded by the same organisation. This is a bit tricky to set up in Webometric Analyst because each collection of articles from a subgroup or the main group and from each field and year must be saved in a separate file, and the files must be named following a specific set of rules. The rules are necessary to help Webometric Analyst to detect the different groups of articles.

For each field and year there is a main "world" file that contains the reference set of articles—normally either a complete collection of all articles from the field and year indexed by Scopus or WoS, or a random sample from this collection. For each field and year there is also one or more additional files for the different groups of articles (e.g., those from a specific research group). Here are the rules for these files and Figure 10.2 gives an example.

- Each field and year must have a "whole world" query file containing the reference set. Its file name for this must end in -world.txt or a standard derivative ending created by Webometric Analyst when used to generate sets of queries. All of the following are valid file name endings:

  ○ -world.txt, -world_ppt.txt, -world_syll.txt, -world_blog.txt, -world_pat.txt, -world_wiki.txt, -world_web.txt or -world_grey.txt

- Each field and year must have one or more files containing queries for the selected groups. The query file names must start the same as the whole world file but replace -world.txt (or -world_ppt.txt, etc.) with -NAME.txt, where NAME can be any identifier.

3403 Food Animals 2011_search_ppt-GroupA.txt
3403 Food Animals 2011_search_ppt-world.txt
3403 Food Animals 2012_search_ppt-GroupA.txt
3403 Food Animals 2012_search_ppt-world.txt
Agriculture 2011_search_ppt-GroupA.txt
Agriculture 2011_search_ppt-world.txt
Agriculture 2012_search_ppt-GroupA.txt
Agriculture 2012_search_ppt-world.txt

Figure 10.2: A set of query files following the standardised group naming convention and ready to input into Webometric Analyst. Four files end in -world.txt and each one includes a complete list of Scopus articles from a single field and year. For each of these four files there is a corresponding file with -world.txt replaced by -GroupA.txt. This is a set of files from a specific group that forms a subset of each of the four world files.

If random samples are used rather than complete world files in order to reduce the numbers of queries to be selected, then the Webometric Analyst option *Replace Search File(s) with a random sample up to a maximum number* can be used from the *Make Searches* menu for this.

Each of the query files must then be submitted separately to Bing in Webometric Analyst. For each file, start Webometric Analyst, select the Web Impact Report option from the start-up wizard, select the file and wait for it to finish. Keep all the files together in the original folder (Figure 10.3). After this, check the results for false matches. If you find any, delete the rows for them from their long results file.

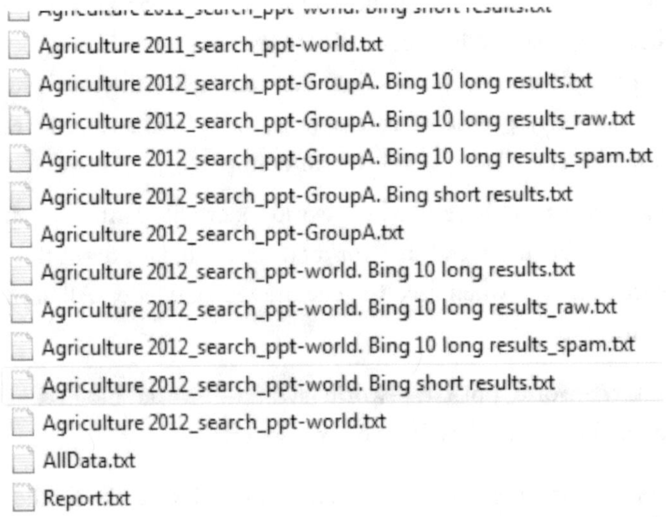

Agriculture 2011_search_ppt-world. Bing short results.txt
Agriculture 2011_search_ppt-world.txt
Agriculture 2012_search_ppt-GroupA. Bing 10 long results.txt
Agriculture 2012_search_ppt-GroupA. Bing 10 long results_raw.txt
Agriculture 2012_search_ppt-GroupA. Bing 10 long results_spam.txt
Agriculture 2012_search_ppt-GroupA. Bing short results.txt
Agriculture 2012_search_ppt-GroupA.txt
Agriculture 2012_search_ppt-world. Bing 10 long results.txt
Agriculture 2012_search_ppt-world. Bing 10 long results_raw.txt
Agriculture 2012_search_ppt-world. Bing 10 long results_spam.txt
Agriculture 2012_search_ppt-world. Bing short results.txt
Agriculture 2012_search_ppt-world.txt
AllData.txt
Report.txt

Figure 10.3: A folder containing the original query files from the previous figure, the extra files generated by Bing searches, and the report Report.txt and a summary of the raw data, AllData.txt.

Once Webometric Analyst has submitted all queries in all of the files to the Bing API, the field- and year-normalised indicators can be calculated. To do this, from the *Report* menu, select the *Calculate MNLCS, gMNCS and NPC for a set of web searches (multiple files with structured names)* menu option and then select the folder containing the above results. It will save a set of indicators into a new file (Figure 10.4). The arithmetic mean of the world-normalised, log-transformed data is recommended as the most robust indicator. Values above 1 indicate scores above the world average. As argued above, the domain counting option is normally preferable.

```
Group file: GroupA. In set: Agriculture 2013
Queries: 147
Arithmetic mean (unique URLs): 0.046000
Arithmetic mean (unique domains): 0.042000
Arithmetic mean (unique sites): 0.030000
Arithmetic mean (unique STLDs): 0.030000
Arithmetic mean (unique TLDs): 0.030000
Proportion non zero (95%CI): 0.030000 (0.018263, 0.048904)
Mean (95%CI) of log (1+unique URLs): 0.026811 (0.012720, 0.040902)
Mean (95%CI) of log (1+unique domains): 0.025424 (0.012140, 0.038709)
Mean (95%CI) of log (1+unique sites): 0.020794 (0.010314, 0.031275)
Mean (95%CI) of log (1+unique STLDs): 0.020794 (0.010314, 0.031275)
Mean (95%CI) of log (1+unique TLDs): 0.020794 (0.010314, 0.031275)
Geometric mean (95%CI) of unique URLs: 0.027173 (0.012801, 0.041750)
Geometric mean (95%CI) of unique domains: 0.025750 (0.012214, 0.039468)
Geometric mean (95%CI) of unique sites: 0.021012 (0.010367, 0.031769)
Geometric mean (95%CI) of unique STLDs: 0.021012 (0.010367, 0.031769)
Geometric mean (95%CI) of unique TLDs: 0.021012 (0.010367, 0.031769)
MNLCS - mean (95%CI) of world normalised log (unique URLs): 3.223308 (1.529245, 4.917371)
MNLCS - mean (95%CI) of world normalised log (1+unique domains): 3.667970 (1.751454,
5.584486)
MNLCS - mean (95%CI) of world normalised log (1+unique sites): 3.000000 (1.487967, 4.512033)
MNLCS - mean (95%CI) of world normalised log (1+unique STLDs): 3.000000 (1.487967, 4.512033)
MNLCS - mean (95%CI) of world normalised log (1+unique TLDs): 3.000000 (1.487967, 4.512033)
NPC - world normalised proportion (95%CI) non-zero [i.e. risk ratio]: 1.000000 (0.985889, 1.014313)
```

Figure 10.4: An extract from Report.txt containing the field-normalised Wikipedia citation indicators calculated for GroupA for Agriculture in 2013. The bottom set is the optimal field- and year-normalized MNLCS calculation, and the domain counting method is usually preferred to avoid duplicate pages in the results. In the above case all matching URLs for each query come from the same site (wikipedia.org) and so the results are identical for sites, STLDs and TLDs.

The above results are available in report.txt for each individual field and year combination. Below them in Report.txt is a table that combines all field/year sets in order to give the main overall results, preceded by a brief description (Figure 10.5). Here, for URL counting, GroupA's MNLCS log-transformed citations are, on average, 1.462 times bigger than the world average, but the difference is not statistically significant because the world average (1) is inside the 95% confidence interval of (0.881,2.163).

The Mean Normalised Log-transformed Citation Scores (MNLCS) in the table below are the best to use to compare the group overall with the world average if there are multiple different world averages (e.g., different fields and/or years).

Group	SampleSize	URLMNLCS	URLLower95Sample	URLUpper95Sample
World	15000	1	0.831697	1.237059
GroupA	1150	1.4617961	0.881288	2.162628

The above set of results shows that, using URL counting, the MNLCS for GroupA is 1.462, with a 95% confidence interval of (0.881,2.163).

Figure 10.5: An extract from Report.txt containing the field-normalised Wikipedia citation indicators calculated for GroupA. Although there are four different GroupA files, each for a different field and year, this report contains combined results for all of them. Webometric Analyst can do this because it has recognised from the filenames that all of the GroupA files are associated with the same group. It has also field- and year-normalised each group separately.

The NPC information for the combined set of fields/years is further down the report (Figure 10.6). In this case 2.33% of GroupA's articles were cited in comparison to a world average of 1.67%. The difference is not statistically significant because the world average is inside the GroupA 95% confidence interval. GroupA's articles have non-zero citations at a NPC ratio of 1.3944 times the world average, although again the world average (1) is inside the GroupA confidence interval of (0.9439,2.0598), so the difference is not statistically significant.

Field equalised proportion non-zero calculations - all group sample sizes are set to the arithmetic mean sample size for sets with at least one publication							
Group	N	AvPropNonzero	Lower95	Upp95	NPC_Ratio	Low95	Upp95
world	15000	0.0167	0.0148	0.0189	1.0000	0.8408	1.1892
GroupA	1150	0.0233	0.0160	0.0337	1.3944	0.9439	2.0598

Figure 10.6: An extract from Report.txt containing the field-normalised Wikipedia proportion cited and NPC indicators calculated for GroupA. Although there are four different GroupA files, each for a different field and year, this report contains combined results for all of them.

10.2   INDICATORS FROM MENDELEY READER DATA

To calculate a set of field-normalised and other indicators for Mendeley data, the procedure, options and output are the same as for web data except that the document information files are needed rather than Bing query files, and Mendeley results files are needed rather than Bing API results. Here are the procedures, mainly echoing the instructions above.

10.2.1 SEPARATE INDICATORS FOR EACH SET OF MENDELEY READERS

The Mendeley reader files must be split by field and year so that each set of articles or books from the same field and year is in a different file. This is important to avoid calculating indicators from collections of articles that mix fields and years. For this only the Mendeley search results files ending in _total85.txt should be used because these contain the main information.

To calculate a set of indicators for Mendeley readers, from the *Reports* menu, select the *Calculate MNLCS and gMNCS for a set of Mendeley API results files (one or more files, each processed separately)* menu option. It will calculate a range of indicators, such as the arithmetic mean, the geometric mean and the arithmetic mean of the log-normalised values for each file separately, saving the results to a plain text file.

10.2.2 FIELD-NORMALISED INDICATORS TO COMPARE SUBGROUPS TO THE WORLD AVERAGE

If a subgroup of documents needs to be compared to a larger group, such as all documents produced by a department against the world average, then the group's documents and world documents must be saved into different files. A standard naming convention is necessary to help Webometric Analyst to detect the different groups of documents. For each field and year there must be a main "world" file that contains the reference set of documents—normally a complete collection of all documents from the field and year indexed by Scopus or WoS. For each field and year there are also one or more additional files for the different groups of documents (e.g., those from a specific research group). Here are the rules for these files. Figure 10.7 gives an example.

- Each set of documents must be in a separate plain text file of publication metadata (see Section 8.2 and 8.3).

- Each field and year must have a whole world file containing the reference set. The file name for this must end in -world.txt.

- Each field and year must have one or more files containing publication information for selected groups. These file names must start the same as the whole world file but replace -world.txt with -NAME.txt, where NAME can be any identifier.

Scopus-BIOC 2013-MRC.txt	Scopus-BIOC 2016-MRC.txt	Scopus-IMMU 2015-world.txt	Scopus-MEDI 2015-MRC.txt
Scopus-BIOC 2013-NIH.txt	Scopus-BIOC 2016-NIH.txt	Scopus-IMMU 2016-MRC.txt	Scopus-MEDI 2015-NIH.txt
Scopus-BIOC 2013-Wellcome.txt	Scopus-BIOC 2016-Wellcome.txt	Scopus-IMMU 2016-Wellcome.txt	Scopus-MEDI 2015-Wellcome.txt
Scopus-BIOC 2013-world.txt	Scopus-BIOC 2016-world.txt	Scopus-IMMU 2016-world.txt	Scopus-MEDI 2015-world.txt
Scopus-BIOC 2014-MRC.txt	Scopus-IMMU 2013-MRC.txt	Scopus-MEDI 2013-MRC.txt	Scopus-MEDI 2016-MRC.txt
Scopus-BIOC 2014-NIH.txt	Scopus-IMMU 2013-Wellcome.txt	Scopus-MEDI 2013-NIH.txt	Scopus-MEDI 2016-NIH.txt
Scopus-BIOC 2014-Wellcome.txt	Scopus-IMMU 2013-world.txt	Scopus-MEDI 2013-Wellcome.txt	Scopus-MEDI 2016-Wellcome.txt
Scopus-BIOC 2014-world.txt	Scopus-IMMU 2014-MRC.txt	Scopus-MEDI 2013-world.txt	Scopus-MEDI 2016-world.txt
Scopus-BIOC 2015-MRC.txt	Scopus-IMMU 2014-Wellcome.txt	Scopus-MEDI 2014-MRC.txt	Scopus-NIH 2013-MRC.txt
Scopus-BIOC 2015-NIH.txt	Scopus-IMMU 2014-world.txt	Scopus-MEDI 2014-NIH.txt	Scopus-NIH 2014-MRC.txt
Scopus-BIOC 2015-Wellcome.txt	Scopus-IMMU 2015-MRC.txt	Scopus-MEDI 2014-Wellcome.txt	Scopus-NIH 2015-MRC.txt
Scopus-BIOC 2015-world.txt	Scopus-IMMU 2015-Wellcome.txt	Scopus-MEDI 2014-world.txt	Scopus-NIH 2016-MRC.txt

Figure 10.7: A set of publication information files following the standardised group naming convention to split by field (BIOC, IMMU, MEDI), year (2013–2016) and group (MRC, NIH, Wellcome) so that these three groups can be compared to the world average. The files are ready to input into Webometric Analyst to calculate Mendeley readers.

After collecting Mendeley readership information from these files with Webometric Analyst, the files created should automatically be given appropriate names, as shown in Figure 10.8 and described below.

- Each set of articles will have a separate Mendeley results file ending in _total85.txt, as well as other associated files.

- Each field and year will have a whole world file containing the reference set and ending in world_pubsFound_total85.txt.

- Each field and year will have one or more files containing results for selected groups. Their file names for the above must start the same as the whole world file but replace - world_pubsFound_total85.txt with - NAME_pubsFound_total85.txt, where NAME can be any identifier.

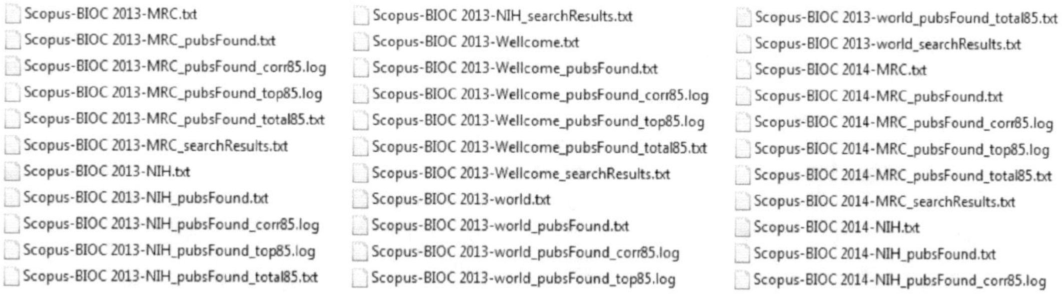

Scopus-BIOC 2013-MRC.txt
Scopus-BIOC 2013-MRC_pubsFound.txt
Scopus-BIOC 2013-MRC_pubsFound_corr85.log
Scopus-BIOC 2013-MRC_pubsFound_top85.log
Scopus-BIOC 2013-MRC_pubsFound_total85.txt
Scopus-BIOC 2013-MRC_searchResults.txt
Scopus-BIOC 2013-NIH.txt
Scopus-BIOC 2013-NIH_pubsFound.txt
Scopus-BIOC 2013-NIH_pubsFound_corr85.log
Scopus-BIOC 2013-NIH_pubsFound_top85.log
Scopus-BIOC 2013-NIH_pubsFound_total85.txt

Scopus-BIOC 2013-NIH_searchResults.txt
Scopus-BIOC 2013-Wellcome.txt
Scopus-BIOC 2013-Wellcome_pubsFound.txt
Scopus-BIOC 2013-Wellcome_pubsFound_corr85.log
Scopus-BIOC 2013-Wellcome_pubsFound_top85.log
Scopus-BIOC 2013-Wellcome_pubsFound_total85.txt
Scopus-BIOC 2013-Wellcome_searchResults.txt
Scopus-BIOC 2013-world.txt
Scopus-BIOC 2013-world_pubsFound.txt
Scopus-BIOC 2013-world_pubsFound_corr85.log
Scopus-BIOC 2013-world_pubsFound_top85.log

Scopus-BIOC 2013-world_pubsFound_total85.txt
Scopus-BIOC 2013-world_searchResults.txt
Scopus-BIOC 2014-MRC.txt
Scopus-BIOC 2014-MRC_pubsFound.txt
Scopus-BIOC 2014-MRC_pubsFound_corr85.log
Scopus-BIOC 2014-MRC_pubsFound_top85.log
Scopus-BIOC 2014-MRC_pubsFound_total85.txt
Scopus-BIOC 2014-MRC_searchResults.txt
Scopus-BIOC 2014-NIH.txt
Scopus-BIOC 2014-NIH_pubsFound.txt
Scopus-BIOC 2014-NIH_pubsFound_corr85.log

Figure 10.8: A set of Mendeley results files generated using Webometric Analyst applied to the set of Scopus files in the figure above. Webometric Analyst will ignore the files ending in .log and _pubsFound.txt when generating the report.

To calculate a range of indicators, from the Webometric Analyst Report menu, select the *Calculate MNLCS and gMNCS for a set of Mendeley API results files (multiple files with structured names)* menu option and then select the folder containing the above files. It will save a set of indicators into a report file (see Figures 10.9, 10.10).

```
Group file: MRC. In set: Scopus-BIOC 2013
Records: 617
Arithmetic mean: 33.047002
Proportion non-zero (95%CI): 0.9740 (0.9582, 0.9839)
Mean (95%CI) of ln(1+raw data): 3.0514 (2.9713, 3.1315)
Geometric mean (95%CI) of raw data: 20.1459 (18.5179, 21.9096)
Mean (95%CI) of world normalised ln(1+raw data)[population version]: 1.6079 (1.5657, 1.6501)
Mean (95%CI) of world normalised ln(1+raw data) [sample version]: 1.6079 (1.5608, 1.6556)
World normalised proportion (95%CI) non-zero [ie risk ratio]: 1.2813 (1.2600, 1.3030)


Group file: NIH. In set: Scopus-BIOC 2013
Records: 10000
Arithmetic mean: 27.511300
Proportion non-zero (95%CI): 0.9535 (0.9491, 0.9574)
Mean (95%CI) of ln(1+raw data): 2.7581 (2.7370, 2.7792)
Geometric mean (95%CI) of raw data: 14.7705 (14.4412, 15.1068)
Mean (95%CI) of world normalised ln(1+raw data) [population version]: 1.4533 (1.4422, 1.4644)
Mean (95%CI) of world normalised ln(1+raw data) [sample version]: 1.4533 (1.4305, 1.4766)
World normalised proportion (95%CI) non-zero [ie risk ratio]: 1.2542 (1.2395, 1.2691)


Group file: Wellcome. In set: Scopus-BIOC 2013
Records: 761
Arithmetic mean: 35.8120
Proportion non-zero (95%CI): 0.981603 (0.9693, 0.9890)
Mean (95%CI) of ln(1+raw data): 3.161463 (3.0923, 3.2305)
Geometric mean (95%CI) of raw data: 22.6051 (21.0291, 24.2938)
Mean (95%CI) of world normalised ln(1+raw data) [population version]: 1.6658 (1.6294, 1.7022)
Mean (95%CI) of world normalised ln(1+raw data)  sample version]: 1.6658 (1.6233, 1.7089)
World normalised proportion (95%CI) non-zero [ie risk ratio]: 1.2912 (1.2725, 1.3101)
```

Figure 10.9: An extract from Report.txt containing the field-normalised Mendeley reader indicators calculated for MRC, NIH and Wellcome for Biochemistry in 2013.

Group	N	MNLCS	Lower95	Upper95
World	119672	1.0000	0.992984	1.007188
MRC	8107	1.8111	1.789951	1.832647
NIH	84563	1.6311	1.620091	1.642531
Wellcome	6044	1.8995	1.875952	1.923527

Group	N	AvPropNonzero	Lower95	Upp95	NPC_Ratio	Low95	Upp95
World	119672	0.6793	0.6766	0.6819	1.0000	0.994	1.005
MRC	8107	0.9027	0.8960	0.9089	1.3288	1.318	1.339
NIH	84563	0.9160	0.9141	0.9178	1.3484	1.342	1.354
Wellcome	6044	0.9151	0.9078	0.9219	1.3471	1.335	1.358

Figure 10.10: An extract from Report.txt containing the field-normalised Mendeley reader indicators calculated for MRC, NIH and Wellcome overall for all years and fields. MNLCS values and confidence intervals are in the upper table, and NPC values and confidence intervals are in the lower table.

10.3   INDICATORS FROM OTHER DATA SOURCES

To calculate a set of field-normalised and other indicators for Google Books, WorldCat library holdings or even Scopus/WoS citation data, the procedure, options and output are the same as for Mendeley except that unused files will not be ignored and must be removed from the folder before processing. Here are the procedures, mainly echoing the instructions above.

10.3.1   SEPARATE INDICATORS FOR EACH FILE OF INDICATOR SCORES

The raw data must be saved in tab-delimited plain text files, with one column containing the figures to be analysed. The files must be split by field and year so that each set of articles or books from the same field and year is in a different file. This is important to avoid calculating indicators from collections that mix fields and years.

To calculate a set of indicators from these raw scores, from the *Reports* menu, select the *Calculate MNLCS and gMNCS for a set of any tab-delimited files (one or more files, each processed separately)* menu option. It will calculate a range of indicators for each file separately, summarising the results in a plain text file, such as the one in Figure 10.1.

10.3.2   FIELD-NORMALISED INDICATORS TO COMPARE SUBGROUPS TO THE WORLD AVERAGE

If a subgroup of articles needs to be compared to a larger group, such as all articles produced by a department against the world average, then the group's documents and world documents must be saved in different files. For each field and year there must a main "world" file that contains the reference set of documents—normally a complete collection of all documents from the field and year indexed by Scopus or WoS or a random sample. For each field and year there must also be one or more additional files for the different groups of articles (e.g., those from a specific research group). Here are the rules for these files.

- Each set must be in a separate file stored within a common folder.

- Each field and year must have a whole world file containing the reference set, and with a file name ending in -world.txt.

- Each field and year must have one or more files containing the data for selected groups. Their file names must start the same as the whole world file but replace -world. txt with -NAME.txt, where NAME can be any identifier.

- All files not following the above rules must be removed from the folder before processing.

To calculate a range of indicators, from the Webometric Analyst *Report* menu, select the *Calculate MNLCS and gMNCS for a set of any tab-delimited files (multiple files with structured names)* menu option and then select the folder containing the above files. The indicators will be saved into a new file (Figures 10.11, 10.12).

```
Group file: MRC. In set: Scopus-BIOC 2013
Records: 617
Arithmetic mean: 14.484603
Proportion non-zero (95%CI): 0.949757 (0.929567, 0.964381)
Mean (95%CI) of ln(1+raw data): 2.252676 (2.172765, 2.332587)
Geometric mean (95%CI) of raw data: 8.513159 (7.782531, 9.304569)
Mean (95%CI) of world normalised ln(1+raw data) [population version]: 1.5036 (1.4503, 1.5570)
Mean (95%CI) of world normalised ln(1+raw data)    [sample version]: 1.5036 (1.4470, 1.5608)
World normalised proportion (95%CI) non-zero [ie risk ratio]: 1.1994 (1.1750, 1.2244)

Group file: NIH. In set: Scopus-BIOC 2013
Records: 10000
Arithmetic mean: 13.575200
Proportion non-zero (95%CI): 0.9513 (0.9469, 0.9553)
Mean (95%CI) of ln(1+raw data): 2.1658 (2.1468, 2.1847)
Geometric mean (95%CI) of raw data: 7.7215 (7.5575, 7.8887)
Mean (95%CI) of world normalised ln(1+raw data) [population version]: 1.4456 (1.4330, 1.4583)
Mean (95%CI) of world normalised ln(1+raw data)    [sample version]: 1.4456 (1.4220, 1.4699)
World normalised proportion (95%CI) non-zero [ie risk ratio]: 1.2014 (1.1883, 1.2147)

Group file: Wellcome. In set: Scopus-BIOC 2013
Records: 761
Arithmetic mean: 14.758213
Proportion non-zero (95%CI): 0.9632 (0.9473, 0.9744)
Mean (95%CI) of ln(1+raw data): 2.2788 (2.2085, 2.3492)
Geometric mean (95%CI) of raw data: 8.765655 (8.102196, 9.477473)
Mean (95%CI) of world normalised ln(1+raw data) [population version]: 1.5211 (1.4742, 1.5681)
Mean (95%CI) of world normalised ln(1+raw data)    [sample version] : 1.5211 (1.4702, 1.5726)
World normalised proportion (95%CI) non-zero [ie risk ratio]: 1.2164 (1.1959, 1.2373)
```

Figure 10.11: An extract from Report.txt containing the field-normalised Scopus citation indicators calculated for MRC, NIH and Wellcome for Biochemistry in 2013.

Group	N	MNLCS	Lower95	Upper95
World	119672	1.0000	0.984809	1.015889
MRC	8107	2.0036	1.954215	2.054196
NIH	84563	1.8396	1.813382	1.867167
Wellcome	6044	1.9677	1.915835	2.020523

Group	N	AvPropNonzero	Lower95	Upp95	NPC_Ratio	Low95	Upp95
World	119672	0.4871	0.4842	0.4899	1.0000	0.991	1.008
MRC	8107	0.7126	0.7026	0.7223	1.4629	1.441	1.485
NIH	84563	0.6909	0.6878	0.6940	1.4185	1.408	1.429
Wellcome	6044	0.7028	0.6912	0.7142	1.4429	1.418	1.468

Figure 10.12: An extract from Report.txt containing the field-normalised Scopus citation indicators calculated for MRC, NIH and Wellcome overall for all years and fields. MNLCS values and confidence intervals are in the upper table and NPC values and confidence intervals are in the lower table.

10.4   SUMMARY

Webometric Analyst contains a range of functions designed to simplify the task of calculating indicator formulae and confidence intervals for web indicator data. The main two are MNLCS and NPC, although Webometric Analyst can also calculate the proportion cited and geometric mean for collections of outputs from a single field and year. Thus, Webometric Analyst can be used to download and process web indicators with the formulae necessary for evaluations of large collections of documents, simplifying and speeding up the whole process.

CHAPTER 11

Conclusions

This book has attempted to lower the threshold to the use of web indicators by putting together in one place the theory, practice and software necessary for appropriately selecting, collecting, analysing and interpreting them. A wide range of web indicators have been proposed to supplement or replace citation counts to support different types of research evaluation. Most indicators derived from the social web offer much earlier evidence of impact, or at least attention, than citations, and are useful for publishers' websites and to help literature searchers. Mendeley reader counts offer relatively early impact evidence and a strong connection to scholarly impact and so are particularly helpful for research evaluations when timeliness is important. Web indicators that offer evidence of educational, informational, commercial, organisational or book-based impact (Table 11.1) are useful for applications when these types of impacts are important, or when evidence is sought of all types of impacts. Many web indicators have low coverage, but these can be useful for highlighting individual high impact outputs and to compare large sets of outputs with the aid of the NPC calculation.

Web indicators are particularly useful for evaluations that need to assess the societal impacts of scholarly work. Such evaluations should not be conducted when there is a possibility of deliberate manipulation of the data and so this rules out typical large-scale research assessment exercises that give advance warning of methods. The possibility of manipulation is not a problem for surprise evaluations when the choice of indicators is not known in advance, as well as for self-evaluations.

Web indicators can be used to support specific impact claims by scholars, particularly if their work has non-academic impacts or if they produce non-standard outputs. On a small scale, honesty statements from authors may reduce the risk of manipulation when web indicators are used to support specific impact claims. Here, the choice of web indicator depends on the type of impact to be assessed and the amount of outputs to assess. Ideally, the web indicators should support a written description of the type of impact claimed.

Table 11.1: Estimated Spearman correlations with citations (WoS or Scopus) and coverage (% of WoS or Scopus articles/books with non-zero values) for web indicators. All correlations are approximate due to differences between years and individual fields. All values are for journal articles, unless books are specified. Data is taken from, or estimated from, the sources cited in the text.

Data source	Overall	Health Sciences	Natural Science	Social Science	Arts and Humanities	Impact Type	Earliest Evidence
Downloads	.9 100%	100%	.4 100%	100%	100%	Usage, academic, educational	1 year
Syllabi		0.5%	1%	.23 10%		Educational	Years
Syllabi-books	.3 38%	.3 24%	.2 35%	.3 45%	.3 56%	Educational	Years
PowerPoint				2%		Educational, academic	Years
Wikipedia	.09	.15 4%	.1 5%	.15 4%	.1 7%	Educational, informational	Years
Wikipedia Books		.35** 25%	.3** 25%	.25** 30%	.3** 48%	Educational, informational	
Grey Literature						Commercial, organisational	Years
Web	.2 100%	100%	100%	100%	100%	Attention	Years
Patents		.15 3%	.2 1%			Commercial	Years
Tweets		.1 13%	.1 7%	.05 9%	-0.3 7%	Attention	Weeks
Mendeley Readers		.4 67%	.4 65%	.45 70%	.35 50%	Academic	1 year
Facebook Posts	.05 12%					Attention	Weeks
Google+ Posts	.03 2%					Attention	Weeks
Blog Posts	.2 6%					Academic	Months
F1000 chg. Clin. Prac.	NA		NA	NA	NA	Health	Months
F1000 Scores	NA		NA	NA	NA	Medical/ academic	Months
Clinical Guide.	NA		NA	NA	NA	Health	Years
Clinical Trials	NA		NA	NA	NA	Health	Years
Book Reviews	29%	.1 29%	.1 29%	.2 25%	.2 31%	Usage, academic, educational	Years
Library Holdings	100%	.1 100%	.1 100%	.15 100%	.15 100%	Usage, academic, educational	Years
Book Sales	100%	0.15 100%	0.15 100%	0.25 100%	0.25 100%	Usage, academic, educational	1 year
Google Books			.25 4%	.5 100%	.5 200%	Academic, educational	4–5 years

* Percentage of WoS or Scopus citations rather than percentage with non-zero values. **Correlation with Google Books citations

11.1   WEB INDICATORS FOR BOOKS

Citations from Google Books form a particularly promising academic impact web indicator for books because they are more numerous than citations from WoS or Scopus and because the natural place for the impact of book-based scholarship is in other books. Some fields publish primarily in books and so are not well represented in citation indexes that do not index a substantial fraction of the world's academic books.

Another book-specific issue relates to attempts to compare the average impact of collections of monographs. Comparisons of indicator values for topically heterogeneous collections of books suffer from the lack of a recognised appropriate subject categorisation scheme for them. This makes it difficult to calculate the world average for benchmarking or normalisation purposes. This, combined with the multiple different audiences and types of impacts of books, means that the problem of generating simple and effective indicators for book-based scholarship is still not fully solved.

11.2   WEB INDICATORS FOR OTHER SCHOLARLY OUTPUTS

Data, software, videos, blogs and images are complex to assess because they are not standardised in size, purpose or intended audience. For example, a simple image editing program might be downloaded by millions of website editors whereas a highly complex protein sequence visualizer might only attract 20 specialist users; it does not make sense to compare these figures. By extension, it would be unfair to compare the average numbers of downloads of software created by one department with the average numbers of downloads of software created by another if they were of different types. This is the underlying cause of the lack of empirical evidence for the value of non-standard outputs in the chapters above. Instead, web indicators for non-standard outputs can be used on an individual basis to support a narrative that makes a claim for the type of impact generated. The role of the indicators here is to strengthen a claim made in the narrative text. The value of the evidence would be enhanced if it could be benchmarked in some way. For example, an author might cite web indicators to claim that their resource had more users than any comparable resource.

11.3   RESPONSIBLY INTERPRETING WEB INDICATORS

The responsible use of web indicators is essential to avoid bad decisions being taken on the basis of misinterpreted data. As mentioned above, since web indicators can be manipulated by users they should not be used in evaluations in which those evaluated have a stake in the outcome and time to manipulate the scores.

Even when manipulation is not likely, all web indicators have flaws so they should not be accepted at face value, even if statistical formulae are used with them to generate confidence intervals. It is always possible that a high value on an indicator is due to its flaws rather than great underlying impact. In addition, the type of impact reflected by a particular indicator may differ in individual cases from that for typical cases and some judgement is needed to interpret them. For example, if an art history book targets a popular audience then its readership data could be taken as societal or cultural impact evidence. Thus, the ideal role for web indicators is to inform but not replace human judgements.

It is important to consider the strength of the evidence provided by a web indicator when using it. This requires a review of academic evidence that evaluates the indicator. This review should be aware that the most common evaluation technique, correlation tests, does not give evidence of any type of non-scholarly impact reflected by the indicator, although this is clear in some cases (e.g., syllabus mentions, patent citations). The review should also take into consideration disciplinary and temporal differences in the strength of an indicator.

Finally, in contexts when web indicators are used in place of human judgements, then their values should always be interpreted cautiously and they should not be used to support strong conclusions. For example, if Mendeley indicators for the UK decreased relative to its international competitors then this would certainly not be proof that an underlying decrease in research impact within the UK had occurred. Instead, this evidence should be combined with other information before a judgement is made.

11.4   THE FUTURE OF WEB INDICATORS

Until recently, web indicators have not been used in evaluations, even when there was no risk of manipulation. This is because the values need to be benchmarked against the world average, or at least against comparable values, in order to be interpreted. The techniques introduced in this book with Webometric Analyst offer a way to solve this problem through the use of software to collect a range of alternative indicator values and to calculate field-normalised scores for evaluations. This should make it much simpler for future evaluators to use alternative indicators, when appropriate. Altmetric data providers are likely to offer more bespoke solutions, including more comprehensive social media data.

If web indicators are more widely used in future then this can change the scholarly landscape by recognising the varied contributions to society that scholars make, including those that have educational, health, commercial and organisational impacts. This would help society and government to recognise the contributions of academia and also individual scholars to be appropriately recognised and rewarded for their useful work. The recognition should also extend to cover the valuable non-standard outputs that many scholars produce, such as datasets, software, blogs and videos.

Bibliobraphy

Abdullah, A. and Thelwall, M. (2014). Can the impact of non-Western academic books be measured? An investigation of Google Books and Google Scholar for Malaysia. *Journal of the Association for Information Science and Technology*, 65(12), 2498–2508. DOI:10.1002/asi.23145. 46

Abramo, G. and D'Angelo, C.A. (2015). The VQR, Italy's second national research assessment: Methodological failures and ranking distortions. *Journal of the Association for Information Science and Technology*, 66(11), 2202-2214. DOI: 10.1002/asi.23323. 67

ACUMEN Portfolio (2014). Guidelines for Good Evaluation Practice (2014). The ACUMEN Consortium. http://research-acumen.eu/wp-content/uploads/D6.14-Good-Evaluation-Practices.pdf. 66

Adie, E. and Roe, W. (2013). Altmetric: enriching scholarly content with article-level discussion and metrics. *Learned Publishing*, 26(1), 11–17. DOI: 10.1087/20130103. 62

Albers, C. (2003). Using the syllabus to document the scholarship of teaching. *Teaching Sociology*, 31(1), 60–72. DOI: 10.2307/3211425.

Alhoori, H. and Furuta, R. (2014). Do altmetrics follow the crowd or does the crowd follow altmetrics? In *Digital Libraries (JCDL), 2014 IEEE/ACM Joint Conference* on (pp. 375–378). Los Alamitos: IEEE Press. DOI: 10.1109/jcdl.2014.6970193. 34, 36, 44, 47, 57

Allen, L., Jones, C., Dolby, K., Lynn, D., and Walport, M. (2009). Looking for landmarks: The role of expert review and bibliometric analysis in evaluating scientific publication outputs. *PLOS ONE*, 4(6), e5910. DOI: 10.1371/journal.pone.0005910. 58

Almind, T. C. and Ingwersen, P. (1997). Informetric analyses on the World Wide Web: Methodological approaches to 'webometrics'. *Journal of Documentation*, 53(4), 404–426. DOI: 10.1108/EUM0000000007205. 7

Alperin, J. P. (2015). Geographic variation in social media metrics: An analysis of Latin American journal articles. *Aslib Journal of Information Management*, 67(3), 289-304. DOI: 10.1108/AJIM-12-2014-0176. 34, 36, 44

Bailey, B. J. R. (1987). Confidence limits to the risk ratio. Biometrics, 201–205. DOI: 10.2307/2531960. 116

Barnes, C. (2015). The Use of Altmetrics as a Tool for Measuring Research Impact. *Australian Academic and Research Libraries*, 46(2), 121–134. DOI: 10.1080/00048623.2014.1003174. 3

Barrett, A. (2005). The information-seeking habits of graduate student researchers in the humanities. *Journal of Academic Librarianship*, 31(4), 324–331. DOI: 10.1016/j.acalib.2005.04.005.

Bar-Ilan, J., Haustein, S., Peters, I., Priem, J., Shema, H., and Terliesner, J. (2012). Beyond citations: Scholars' visibility on the social Web. *17th International Conference on Science and Technology Indicators (STI2012), Science-Metrix and OST*, Montreal (pp. 98–109).

Becher, T. and Trowler, P. R. (2001). *Academic Tribes and Territories* (2 ed.). Buckinghamp, UK: Open University Press. 107

Bollen, J., Van de Sompel, H., Smith, J. A., and Luce, R. (2005). Toward alternative metrics of journal impact: A comparison of download and citation data. *Information Processing and Management*, 41(6), 1419–1440. DOI: 10.1016/j.ipm.2005.03.024. 73

Bornmann, L. and Haunschild, R. (2016). Normalization of Mendeley reader impact on the reader-and paper-side: A comparison of the mean discipline normalized reader score (MDNRS) with the mean normalized reader score (MNRS) and bare reader counts. *Journal of Informetrics*, 10(3), 776–788. DOI: 10.1016/j.joi.2016.04.015. 111

Bornmann, L. and Leydesdorff, L. (2013). The validation of (advanced) bibliometric indicators through peer assessments: A comparative study using data from InCites and F1000. *Journal of Informetrics*, 7(2), 286–291. DOI: 10.1016/j.joi.2012.12.003. 58

Brody, T., Harnad, S., and Carr, L. (2006). Earlier web usage statistics as predictors of later citation impact. *Journal of the American Society for Information Science and Technology*, 57(8), 1060–1072. DOI: 10.1002/asi.20373. 27

Brooks, T. A. (1986). Evidence of complex citer motivations. *Journal of the American Society for Information Science*, 37, 34–36. DOI: 10.1002/asi.4630370106. 18

Case, D. O. and Higgins, G. M. (2000). How can we investigate citation behaviour? A study of reasons for citing literature in communication. *Journal of the American Society for Information Science*, 51(7), 635–645. DOI: 10.1002/(SICI)1097-4571(2000)51:7<635::AID-ASI6>3.0.CO;2-H. 18

Champion, D. J. and Morris, M. F. (1973). A content analysis of book reviews in the AJS, ASR, and Social Forces. *American Journal of Sociology*, 78(5), 1256–1265. DOI: 10.1086/225431. 37

Chen, K. H., Tang, M. C., Wang, C. M., and Hsiang, J. (2015). Exploring alternative metrics of scholarly performance in the social sciences and humanities in Taiwan. *Scientometrics*, 102(1), 97–112. DOI: 10.1007/s11192-014-1420-6. 54

Colquhoun, D. and Plested, A. (2014). Scientists don't count: why you should ignore altmetrics and other bibliometric nightmares. Available: http://www.dcscience.net/?p=6369. 3

Contopoulos-Ioannidis, D. G., Ntzani, E. E., and Ioannidis, J. P. (2003). Translation of highly promising basic science research into clinical applications. *The American Journal of Medicine*, 114(6), 477–484. DOI: 10.1016/S0002-9343(03)00013-5. 59

Costas, R., Zahedi, Z., and Wouters, P. (2015a). The thematic orientation of publications mentioned on social media: large-scale disciplinary comparison of social media metrics with citations. *Aslib Journal of Information Management*, 67(3), 260–288. DOI: 10.1108/AJIM-12-2014-0173. 44

Costas, R., Zahedi, Z., and Wouters, P. (2015b). Do "altmetrics" correlate with citations? Extensive comparison of altmetric indicators with citations from a multidisciplinary perspective. *Journal of the Association for Information Science and Technology*, 66(10), 2003–2019. DOI: 10.1002/asi.23309. 34, 35, 36, 44

Cronin, B., Snyder, H., and Atkins, H. (1997). Comparative citation rankings of authors in monographic and journal literature: A study of sociology. *Journal of Documentation*, 53(3), 263–273. DOI: 10.1108/EUM0000000007200. 8

Cronin, B. and Sugimoto, C. R. (eds.) (2014). *Beyond Bibliometrics: Harnessing Multidimensional Indicators of Scholarly Impact*. Cambridge, MA: MIT Press. 10

Csardi, G. and Nepusz, T. (2006). The igraph software package for complex network research. *InterJournal, Complex Systems*, 1695(5), 1–9. 29

Desai, T., Shariff, A., Shariff, A., Kats, M., Fang, X., et al. (2012). Tweeting the meeting: An in-depth analysis of Twitter activity at Kidney Week 2011. *PLOS ONE* 7(7), e40253. DOI:10.1371/journal.pone.0040253. 13

Dinsmore, A., Allen, L., and Dolby, K. (2014). Alternative perspectives on impact: The potential of ALMs and altmetrics to inform funders about research impact. *PLoS Biol*, 12(11), e1002003. DOI: 10.1371/journal.pbio.1002003. 72

DORA (2013). San Francisco Declaration on Research Assessment. http://www.embo.org/news/press-releases/2013/san-francisco-declaration-on-research-assessment. 73

Duin, D., King, D., and van den Besselaar, P. (2012). Identifying audiences of e-infrastructures-tools for measuring impact. *PLOS ONE*, 7(12), e50943. DOI: 10.1371/journal.pone.0050943. 40

Elsevier (2013). International Comparative Performance of the UK Research Base—2013. https://www.gov.uk/government/publications/performance-of-the-uk-research-baseinternational-comparison-2013

Eyre-Walker, A. and Stoletzki, N. (2013). The assessment of science: The relative merits of post-publication review, the impact factor, and the number of citations. *PLoS Biol,,* 11(10), e1001675. DOI: 10.1371/journal.pbio.1001675. 58

Eysenbach, G. (2011). Can tweets predict citations? Metrics of social impact based on Twitter and correlation with traditional metrics of scientific impact. *Journal of Medical Internet Research*, 13(4), e123. DOI: 10.2196/jmir.2012. 35

Fairclough, R. and Thelwall, M. (2015). National research impact indicators from Mendeley readers. *Journal of Informetrics*, 9(4), 845–859. DOI: 10.1016/j.joi.2015.08.003. 73, 110

Fenner, M. (2013). What can article-level metrics do for you? *PLoS Biology,* 11(10), e1001687. DOI: 10.1371/journal.pbio.1001687. 44

Fieller, E.C. (1954). Some problems in interval estimation. *Journal of the Royal Statistical Society Series B*, 16(2), 175–185. 112

Garand, J.C. and Giles, M.W. (2011). Ranking scholarly publishers in political science: An alternative approach. *PS: Political Science and Politics*, 44(2), 375–383. DOI: 10.1017/s1049096511000229. 50

Garfield, E. (1999). Journal impact factor: a brief review. *Canadian Medical Association Journal*, 161(8), 979–980. 7, 73

Giménez-Toledo, E., Tejada-Artigas, C., and Mañana-Rodríguez, J. (2013). Evaluation of scientific books' publishers in social sciences and humanities: Results of a survey. *Research Evaluation*, 22(1), 64–77. DOI: 10.1093/reseval/rvs036. 50

Gingras, Y. (2014). Criteria for evaluating indicators. In: Cronin, B., and Sugimoto, C. R. (eds.) (2014). *Beyond Bibliometrics: Harnessing Multidimensional Indicators of Scholarly Impact*. Cambridge, MA: MIT Press (pp. 109–125). 72

Glänzel, W. and Schoepflin, U. (1999). A bibliometric study of reference literature in the sciences and social sciences. *Information Processing and Management*, 35(1), 31–44. DOI: 10.1016/S0306-4573(98)00028-4.

Grant, J., Cottrell, R., Cluzeau, F., and Fawcett, G. (2000). Evaluating "payback" on biomedical research from papers cited in clinical guidelines: Applied bibliometric study. *Bmj*, 320(7242), 1107–1111. DOI: 10.1136/bmj.320.7242.1107. 59

Gray, R. (2015). Has the Research Excellence Framework killed creativity? *Journal of Psychiatric and Mental Health Nursing*, 22(3), 155–156. DOI: 10.1111/jpm.12217. 1

Gunn, W. (2013). Social signals reflect academic impact: What it means when a scholar adds a paper to Mendeley. *Information Standards Quarterly*, 25(2), 33–39. DOI: 10.3789/is-qv25no2.2013.06. 43

Haran, B. and Poliakoff, M. (2011). The periodic table of videos. *Science*, 332(6033), 1046–1047. DOI: 10.1126/science.1196980. 9

Halevi, G. and Moed, H. F. (2014). Usage patterns of scientific journals and their relationship with citations. Context Counts: Pathways to Master Big and Little Data, 241–251. 27

Halevi, G., Nicolas, B., and Bar-Ilan, J. (2016). The complexity of measuring the impact of books. *Publishing Research Quarterly*, 1–14. DOI: 10.1007/s12109-016-9464-5. 8

Haustein, S., Bowman, T. D., Holmberg, K., Peters, I., and Larivière, V. (2014a). Astrophysicists on Twitter: An in-depth analysis of tweeting and scientific publication behavior. *Aslib Journal of Information Management*, 66(3), 279–296. DOI: 10.1108/AJIM-09-2013-0081. 33

Haustein, S., Bowman, T. D., Holmberg, K., Tsou, A., Sugimoto, C. R., and Larivière, V. (2016). Tweets as impact indicators: Examining the implications of automated "bot" accounts on Twitter. *Journal of the Association for Information Science and Technology*, 67(1), 232–238. DOI: 10.1002/asi.23456. 33

Haustein, S., Larivière, V., Thelwall, M., Amyot, D., and Peters, I. (2014b). Tweets vs. Mendeley readers: How do these two social media metrics differ? *IT-Information Technology*, 56(5), 207–215. DOI: 10.1515/itit-2014-1048. 35, 44

Haustein, S. and Siebenlist, T. (2011). Applying social bookmarking data to evaluate journal usage. *Journal of Informetrics*, 5(3), 446–457. DOI: 10.1016/j.joi.2011.04.002. 73

HEFCE (2015). The metric tide: Correlation analysis of REF2014 scores and metrics. Supplementary Report II to the Independent review of the role of metrics in research assessment and management. Hefce. http://www.hefce.ac.uk/media/HEFCE,2014/Content/Pubs/Independentresearch/2015/The,Metric,Tide/2015_metrictideS2.pdf. 27, 35, 45

Helic, H., Strohmaier, M., Trattner, C., Muhr, M., and Lerman, K. (2011). Pragmatic evaluation of folksonomies. *Proceedings of the 20th International Conference on World Wide Web (WWW2011)* (pp. 417–426). New York, NY: ACM. DOI: 10.1145/1963405.1963465. 19

Hicks, D., Wouters, P., Waltman, L., de Rijcke, S., and Rafols, I. (2015). The Leiden Manifesto for research metrics. *Nature*, 520, 429–431. DOI: 10.1038/520429a. 69

Hoffmann, C. P., Lutz, C., and Meckel, M. (2015). A relational altmetric? Network centrality on ResearchGate as an indicator of scientific impact. *Journal of the Association for Information Science and Technology*, 67(4), 765–775. DOI: 10.1002/asi.23423. 28

Holmberg, K. and Thelwall, M. (2014). Disciplinary differences in Twitter scholarly communication, *Scientometrics*, 101(2), 1027–1042. DOI: 10.1007/s11192-014-1229-3.

Holmberg, K. J. (2015). *Altmetrics for Information Professionals: Past, Present and Future.* Chandos Publishing. 7, 10, 62, 74

Hubbard, D. W. (2014). *How to Measure Anything: Finding the Value of Intangibles in Business* (3 ed.). Hoboken, NJ: John Wiley and Sons. 5

Hyland, K. (1999). Academic attribution: Citation and the construction of disciplinary knowledge. *Applied Linguistics*, 20(3), 341–367. DOI: 10.1093/applin/20.3.341.

Hyland, K. (2004). *Disciplinary Discourses: Social Interactions in Academic Writing.* Ann Arbor, MI: University of Michigan Press. DOI: 10.3998/mpub.6719. 107

Jaffe, A., Trajtenberg, M., and Fogarty, M. (2000). The meaning of patent citations: Report on the NBER/Case-Western Reserve Survey of Patentees. *NBER Working Papers No. 7631.* http://www.nber.org/papers/w7631.pdf. 48

Jiang, J., He, D., and Ni, C. (2013). The correlations between article citation and references' impact measures: What can we learn? Proceedings of the American Society for Information Science and Technology, 50(1), 1–4. DOI:10.1002/meet.14505001162. 45

Kousha, K., Thelwall, M., and Abdoli, M. (in press). Goodreads reviews to assess the wider impacts of books. *Journal of the Association for Information Science and Technology.* 37, 46, 56

Kousha, K., Thelwall, M., and Rezaie, S. (2010a). Using the web for research evaluation: The integrated online impact indicator. *Journal of Informetrics*, 4(1), 124–135. DOI: 10.1016/j.joi.2009.10.003. 55

Kousha, K., Thelwall, M., and Rezaie, S. (2010b). Can the impact of scholarly images be assessed online? An exploratory study using image identification technology, *Journal of the American Society for Information Science and Technology*, 61(9), 1734–1744. DOI: 10.1002/asi.21370. 30

Kousha, K., Thelwall, M., and Rezaie, S. (2011). Assessing the citation impact of books: The role of Google Books, Google Scholar and Scopus. *Journal of the American Society for Information Science and Technology*, 62(11) 2147–2164. DOI: 10.1002/asi.21608. 46

Kousha, K. and Thelwall, M. (2007). Google scholar citations and Google Web/URL citations: A multi-discipline exploratory analysis. *Journal of the American Society for Information Science and Technology*, 58(7), 1055–1065. DOI: 10.1002/asi.20584. 15, 25

Kousha, K. and Thelwall, M. (2008). Assessing the impact of disciplinary research on teaching: An automatic analysis of online syllabuses. *Journal of the American Society for Information Science and Technology*, 59(13), 2060–2069. DOI: 10.1002/asi.20920. 54

Kousha, K. and Thelwall, M. (2009). Google book search: Citation analysis for social science and the humanities. *Journal of the American Society for Information Science and Technology*, 60(8), 1537–1549. DOI: 10.1002/asi.21085. 46

Kousha, K. and Thelwall, M. (2015a). An automatic method for extracting citations from Google Books. *Journal of the Association for Information Science and Technology*, 66(2), 309–320. DOI: 10.1002/asi.23170. 45, 46

Kousha, K. and Thelwall, M. (2015b). Alternative metrics for book impact assessment: Can Choice reviews be a useful source? In *Proceedings of the 15th International Conference On Scientometrics and Informetrics* (pp. 59–70). 37, 38

Kousha, K. and Thelwall, M. (2016a). Can Amazon.com reviews help to assess the wider impacts of books? *Journal of the Association for Information Science and Technology*, 67(3), 566–581. DOI: 10.1002/asi.23404. 32, 37, 38, 39, 40, 44, 46

Kousha, K. and Thelwall, M. (in press-a). An automatic method for assessing the teaching impact of books from online academic syllabi. *Journal of the Association for Information Science and Technology*. DOI: 10.1002/asi.23542. 54

Kousha, K. and Thelwall, M. (in press-b). Patent citation analysis with Google. *Journal of the Association for Information Science and Technology*. DOI: 10.1002/asi.23608. 48

Kousha, K. and Thelwall, M. (in press-c). Are Wikipedia citations important evidence of the impact of scholarly articles and books? *Journal of the Association for Information Science and Technology*. DOI: 10.1002/asi.23694. 55, 56, 122

Kovács, B. and Sharkey, A. J. (2014). The paradox of publicity how awards can negatively affect the evaluation of quality. *Administrative Science Quarterly*, 59(1), 1–33. DOI: 10.1177/0001839214523602. 37

Kurtz, M. J., Eichhorn, G., Accomazzi, A., Grant, C., Demleitner, M., Murray, S. S., Martimbeau, N., and Elwell, B. (2005). The bibliometric properties of article readership information. *Journal of the American Society for Information Science and Technology*, 56(2), 111–128. DOI: 10.1002/asi.20096. 27

Kurtz, M. J. and Bollen, J. (2010). Usage bibliometrics. *Annual Review of Information Science and Technology*, 44, 3–64. DOI: 10.1002/aris.2010.1440440108. 8, 23

Kurtz, M. J. and Henneken, E. A. (in press). Measuring metrics-a 40-year longitudinal cross-validation of citations, downloads, and peer review in astrophysics. *Journal of the Association for Information Science and Technology*. DOI: 10.1002/asi.23689. 27

Lancho-Barrantes, B. S., Guerrero Bote, V. P., Rodríguez, Z. C., and de Moya Anegón, F. (2012). Citation flows in the zones of influence of scientific collaborations. *Journal of the American Society for Information Science and Technology*, 63(3), 481–489. DOI: 10.1002/asi.21682. 45

Lazarsfeld, P. F. (1958). Evidence and inference in social research. *Daedalus*, 87(4), 99–130. 5, 14

Lee, C., Sugimoto, C. R., and Zhang, G. (2013). Bias in peer review. *Journal of American Society for Information Science and Technology*, 64(1), 2–17. DOI: 10.1002/asi.22784. 15

Li, X., Thelwall, M., and Giustini, D. (2012). Validating online reference managers for scholarly impact measurement. *Scientometrics*, 91(2), 461–471. DOI: 10.1007/s11192-011-0580-x. 15, 44, 45

Li, X. and Thelwall, M. (2012). F1000, Mendeley and traditional bibliometric indicators. In *Proceedings of the 17th International Conference on Science and Technology Indicators*. (Vol. 2, pp. 451–551). 58

Lin, J. and Fenner, M. (2013). Altmetrics in evolution: defining and redefining the ontology of article-level metrics. *Information Standards Quarterly*, 25(2), 20–26. DOI: 10.3789/isqv25no2.2013.04. 61

Linmans, A. J. M. (2010). Why with bibliometrics the humanities does not need to be the weakest link. *Scientometrics*, 83(2), 337–354. DOI: 10.1007/s11192-009-0088-9.

MacRoberts, M. H. and MacRoberts, B. R. (1989). Problems of citation analysis: A critical review. *Journal of the American Society for Information Science*, 40(5), 342–349. DOI: 10.1002/(SICI)1097-4571(198909)40:5<342::AID-ASI7>3.0.CO;2-U. 2

MacRoberts, M. H. and MacRoberts, B. R. (1996). Problems of citation analysis. *Scientometrics*, 36(3), 435–444. DOI: 10.1007/BF02129604. 4, 13, 15

Maflahi, N. and Thelwall, M. (2016). When are readership counts as useful as citation counts? Scopus versus Mendeley for LIS journals. *Journal of the Association for Information Science and Technology*, 67(1), 191–199. DOI: 10.1002/asi.23369. 44

Marcus, A. and Oransky, I. (2011). Science publishing: The paper is not sacred. *Nature*, 480, 449–450. DOI: 10.1038/480449a. 13

Merton, R. K. (1973). *The Sociology of Science. Theoretical and Empirical Investigations*. Chicago: University of Chicago Press. 2

Metz, P. and Stemmer, J. (1996). A reputational study of academic publishers. *College and Research Libraries*, 57(3), 234–247. DOI: 10.5860/crl_57_03_234. 50

Meyer, E. T. and Schroeder, R. (2015). *Knowledge Machines: Digital Transformations of the Sciences and Humanities*. Cambridge, MA: MIT Press. 1

Meyer, M. (2000). Does science push technology? Patents citing scientific literature. *Research Policy*, 29(3), 409–434. DOI: 10.1016/S0048-7333(99)00040-2. 48

Miller, G. (2016). Making data accessible: The Dryad experience. *Toxicological Sciences*, 149(1), 2–3. DOI: 10.1093/toxsci/kfv238. 29

Moed, H. F. and Halevi, G. (2015). Multidimensional assessment of scholarly research impact. *Journal of the Association for Information Science and Technology*, 66(10), 1988–2002. DOI: 10.1002/asi.23314. 68

Moed, H. F. (2005). *Citation Analysis in Research Evaluation*. New York: Springer. 2, 13

Mohammadi, E., Thelwall, M., Haustein, S., and Larivière, V. (2015). Who reads research articles? An altmetrics analysis of Mendeley user categories. *Journal of the Association for Information Science and Technology*, 66(9), 1832–1846. DOI: 10.1002/asi.23286. 19, 44, 45

Mohammadi, E., Thelwall, M., and Kousha, K. (2016). Can Mendeley bookmarks reflect readership? A survey of user motivations. *Journal of the Association for Information Science and Technology*, 67(5), 1198–1209. DOI:10.1002/asi.23477. 18, 45

Mohammadi, E. and Thelwall, M. (2013). Assessing non-standard article impact using F1000 labels. *Scientometrics*, 97(2), 383–395. DOI: 10.1007/s11192-013-0993-9. 58

Mohammadi, E. and Thelwall, M. (2014). Mendeley readership altmetrics for the social sciences and humanities: Research evaluation and knowledge flows. *Journal of the Association for Information Science and Technology*, 65(8), 1627–1638. DOI: 10.1002/asi.23071. 44

Neuendorf, K. (2002). *The Content Analysis Guidebook*. London: Sage. 18

Neumann, R. (2001). Disciplinary differences and university teaching. *Studies in Higher Education*, 26(2), 135–146. DOI: 10.1080/03075070120052071. 53

Neylon, C. and Wu, S. (2009). Article-level metrics and the evolution of scientific impact. *PLoS Biol*, 7(11), e1000242. DOI: 10.1371/journal.pbio.1000242. 61

Nielsen, F. A. (2007). Scientific citations in Wikipedia. First Monday, 12(8). http://ojs-prod-lib.cc.uic.edu/ojs/index.php/fm/article/view/1997. DOI: 10.5210/fm.v12i8.1997. 55, 56

Owens, B. (2013). Judgement day. *Nature*, 502(7471), 288–290. DOI: 10.1038/502288a. 1

Piwowar, H. A., Day, R. S., and Fridsma, D. B. (2007). Sharing detailed research data is associated with increased citation rate. *PLOS ONE*, 2(3), e308. DOI: 10.1371/journal.pone.0000308. 31

Priem, J., Taraborelli, D., Groth, P., and Neylon, C. (2011). Altmetrics: a manifesto. Available: http://altmetrics.org/manifesto/. 7

Priem, J., Piwowar, H.A., and Hemminger, B.M. (2012). Altmetrics in the wild: using social media to explore scholarly impact. Available: http://arxiv.org/abs/1203.4745v1

Priem, J. and Costello, K. L. (2010). How and why scholars cite on Twitter. *Proceedings of the American Society for Information Science and Technology (ASIST 2010)* (pp. 1–4) DOI: 10.1002/meet.14504701201. 17, 18

Procter, R., Williams, R., Stewart, J., Poschen, M., Snee, H., Voss, A., and Asgari-Targhi, M. (2010). Adoption and use of Web 2.0 in scholarly communications. *Philosophical Transactions of the Royal Society A*, 368 (1926), 4039–4056. 19

Seglen, P.O. (1998). Citation rates and journal impact factors are not suitable for evaluation of research. *ACTA Orthopaedica Scandinavica*, 69(3), 224–229. DOI: 10.3109/17453679809000920. 13, 66

SENSE (2009). Sense ranking of academic publishers. http://www.sense.nl/gfx_content/documents/ABCDE-indeling%20Scientific%20Publishers%20SENSE_approved_May_2009.pdf. 50

Shema, H., Bar-Ilan, J., and Thelwall, M. (2012). Research blogs and the discussion of scholarly information. *PLOS ONE*, 7(5), e35869. DOI: 10.1371/journal.pone.0035869. 13

Shema, H., Bar-Ilan, J., and Thelwall, M. (2014). Do blog citations correlate with a higher number of future citations? Research blogs as a potential source for alternative metrics. *Journal of the Association for Information Science and Technology*, 65(5), 1018–1027. DOI: 10.1002/asi.23037. 47

Shema, H., Bar-Ilan, J., and Thelwall, M. (2015). How is research blogged? A content analysis approach. *Journal of the Association for Information Science and Technology*, 66(6), 1136–1149. DOI: 10.1002/asi.23239. 47

Shuai, X., Pepe, A., and Bollen, J. (2012). How the scientific community reacts to newly submitted preprints: Article downloads, Twitter mentions, and citations. *PLOS ONE*, 7(11), e47523. DOI: 10.1371/journal.pone.0047523. 35

Stone, S. (1982). Humanities scholars: information needs and uses. *Journal of Documentation*, 38(4), 292–313. DOI: 10.1108/eb026734. 8

Sud, P. and Thelwall, M. (2014). Evaluating altmetrics. *Scientometrics*, 98(2), 1131–1143. DOI: 10.1007/s11192-013-1117-2.

Sugimoto, C.R. and Thelwall, M. (2013). Scholars on soap boxes: Science communication and dissemination via TED videos. *Journal of the American Society for Information Science and Technology*, 64(4), 663–674. DOI: 10.1002/asi.22764. 30, 32

Tattersall, A. (ed.) (2016). *Altmetrics: A Practical Guide for Librarians, Researchers and Academics*. London, UK: Facet Publishing. 74

Thelwall, M., Kousha, K., Dinsmore, A. and Dolby, K. (2016). Alternative metric indicators for funding scheme evaluations. *Aslib Journal of Information Management*, 68(1), 2–18. DOI: 10.1108/AJIM-09-2015-0146. 72

Thelwall, M., Haustein, S., Larivière, V., and Sugimoto, C. (2013a). Do altmetrics work? Twitter and ten other candidates. *PLOS ONE*, 8(5), e64841. DOI: 10.1371/journal.pone.0064841. 34, 35, 36, 117

Thelwall, M. and Kousha, K. (2008). Online presentations as a source of scientific impact? An analysis of PowerPoint files citing academic journals. *Journal of the American Society for Information Science and Technology*, 59(5), 805–815. DOI: 10.1002/asi.20803. 15, 55

Thelwall, M. and Kousha, K. (2015). ResearchGate: Disseminating, communicating and measuring scholarship? *Journal of the Association for Information Science and Technology*, 66(5). 876–889. DOI: 10.1002/asi.23236. 28

Thelwall, M. and Kousha, K. (2016a). Academic software downloads from Google Code: Useful usage indicators? *Information Research*, 21(1), paper 709. 29, 31, 117

Thelwall, M. and Kousha, K. (2016b). Figshare: A universal repository for academic resource sharing? *Online Information Review*, 40(3), 333–346. DOI: 10.1108/OIR-06-2015-0190. 29

Thelwall, M. and Kousha, K. (in press-a). ResearchGate articles: Age, discipline, audience size and impact. *Journal of the Association for Information Science and Technology*. DOI: 10.1002asi.23675. 28

Thelwall, M. and Kousha, K. (in press-b). Are citations from clinical trials evidence of higher impact research? An analysis of clinicaltrials.gov. *Scientometrics*. DOI: 10.1007/s11192-016-2112-1. 59

Thelwall, M. and Maflahi, N. (2015). Are scholarly articles disproportionately read in their own country? An analysis of Mendeley readers. *Journal of the Association for Information Science and Technology*, 66(6), 1124–1135. DOI: 10.1002/asi.23252. 45

Thelwall, M. and Maflahi, N. (2016). Guideline references and academic citations as evidence of the clinical value of health research. *Journal of the Association for Information Science and Technology*, 67(4), 960-966. DOI: 10.1002/asi.23432. 59

Thelwall, M. and Sud, P. (2016). National, disciplinary and temporal variations in the extent to which articles with more authors have more impact: Evidence from a geometric field normalised citation indicator. *Journal of Informetrics*, 10(1), 48–61. DOI: 10.1016/j. joi.2015.11.007. 111

Thelwall, M. and Sud, P. (in press). Mendeley readership counts: An investigation of temporal and disciplinary differences. *Journal of the Association for Information Science and Technology*. DOI: 10.1002/asi.23559. 44, 107

Thelwall, M., Tsou, A., Weingart, S., Holmberg, K., and Haustein, S. (2013b). Tweeting links to academic articles, *Cybermetrics*, 17(1), http://www.scit.wlv.ac.uk/~cm1993/papers/TweetingLinksAcademicArticles.pdf. 13, 18, 33, 75

Thelwall, M. and Wilson, P. (2016). Mendeley readership altmetrics for medical articles: An analysis of 45 fields, *Journal of the Association for Information Science and Technology*, 67(8), 1962–1972. DOI: 10.1002/asi.23501. 44, 110

Thelwall, M. (2009). *Introduction to Webometrics: Quantitative Web Research for the Social Sciences*. San Rafael, CA: Morgan and Claypool. DOI: 10.2200/S00176ED1V01Y200903ICR004. 10

Thelwall, M. (2016a). The discretised lognormal and hooked power law distributions for complete citation data: Best options for modelling and regression. *Journal of Informetrics*, 10(2), 336-346. DOI: 10.1016/j.joi.2015.12.007.

Thelwall, M. (2016b). The precision of the arithmetic mean, geometric mean and percentiles for citation data: An experimental simulation modelling approach. *Journal of Informetrics*, 10(1), 110–123. DOI: 10.1016/j.joi.2015.12.001. 113

Thelwall, M. (2016c). Are the discretised lognormal and hooked power law distributions plausible for citation data? *Journal of Informetrics*, 10(2), 454–470. DOI: 10.1016/j.joi.2016.03.001. 110

Thelwall, M. (2016d). Interpreting correlations between citation counts and other indicators. *Scientometrics*, 108(1), 337-347. DOI: 10.1007/s11192-016-1973-7. 17

Thelwall, M. (submitted). Two practical field normalised alternative indicator formulae for research evaluation. 112, 116

Tijssen, R. J. W., Buter, R. K., and Van Leeuwen, T. N. (2000). Technological relevance of science: An assessment of citation linkages between patents and research papers. *Scientometrics*, 47(2), 389–412. DOI: 10.1023/A:1005603513439. 48

Torres-Salinas, D. and Moed, H. F. (2009). Library catalog analysis as a tool in studies of social sciences and humanities: An exploratory study of published book titles in economics. *Journal of Informetrics*, 3(1), 9–26. DOI: 10.1016/j.joi.2008.10.002. 38

Torres-Salinas, D., Robinson-García, N., Jiménez-Contreras, E. and Delgado López-Cózar, E. (2012). Towards a 'Book Publishers Citation Reports'. First approach using the 'Book Citation Index'. *Revista Española de Documentación Científica*, 35(4), 615–620. DOI:10.3989/redc.2012.4.1010. 50

Torres-Salinas, D., Robinson-Garcia, N., Campanario, J. M., and Delgado Lopez-Cozar, E. (2014). Coverage, field specialisation and the impact of scientific publishers indexed in the Book Citation Index. *Online Information Review*, 38(1), 24–42. DOI: 10.1108/OIR-10-2012-0169. 121

Van Noorden, R. (2014). Online collaboration: Scientists and the social network. *Nature*, 512(7513), 126–129. DOI: 10.1038/512126a. 28

van Raan, A.F.J. (1998). In matters of quantitative studies of science the fault of theorists is offering too little and asking too much. *Scientometrics*, 43(1), 129–148. DOI: 10.1007/BF02458401. 2

Vaughan, L. and Huysen, K. (2002). Relationship between links to journal Websites and impact factors, *ASLIB Proceedings* 54(6), 356–361. DOI: 10.1108/00012530210452555. 15

Vaughan, L. and Shaw, D. (2003). Bibliographic and web citations: What is the difference? *Journal of the American Society for Information Science and Technology*, 54(14), 1313–1322. DOI: 10.1002/asi.10338. 15, 25

Vaughan, L. and Shaw, D. (2005). Web citation data for impact assessment: A comparison of four science disciplines. *Journal of the American Society for Information Science and Technology*, 56(10), 1075–1087. DOI: 10.1002/asi.20199. 15, 25

Verleysen, F. T. and Engels, T. C. (2013). A label for peer-reviewed books. *Journal of the American Society for Information Science and Technology*, 64(2), 428–430. DOI: 10.1002/asi.22836. 50

Waltman, L., Calero-Medina, C., Kosten, J., Noyons, E., Tijssen, R. J., Eck, N. J., van Leeuwen, T. N., van Raan, A. F. J., Visser, M. S., and Wouters, P. (2012). The Leiden Ranking 2011/2012: Data collection, indicators, and interpretation. *Journal of the American Society for Information Science and Technology*, 63(12), 2419–2432. DOI: 10.1002/asi.22708. 71

Waltman, L. and Costas, R. (2014). F1000 recommendations as a potential new data source for research evaluation: a comparison with citations. *Journal of the Association for Information Science and Technology*, 65(3), 433–445. DOI: 10.1002/asi.23040. 57, 58

Waltman, L. and Schreiber, M. (2013). On the calculation of percentile-based bibliometric indicators. *Journal of the American Society for Information Science and Technology*, 64(2), 372–379. DOI: 10.1002/asi.22775. 69

Waltman, L., van Eck, N. J., van Leeuwen, T. N., Visser, M. S., and van Raan, A. F. (2011). Towards a new crown indicator: Some theoretical considerations. *Journal of Informetrics*, 5(1), 37–47. DOI: 10.1016/j.joi.2010.08.001. 7, 69, 111, 113

Weller, K., Dornstädter, R., Freimanis, R., Klein, R. N., and Perez, M. (2010). Social software in academia: Three studies on users' acceptance of web 2.0 services. *Proceedings of the 2nd Web Science Conference (WebSci10)*, Retrieved May 29, 2013 from: http://www.phil-fak.uni-duesseldorf.de/fileadmin/Redaktion/Institute/Informationswissenschaft/weller/websci10_submission_62.pdf. 19

Wennerås, C. and Wold, A. (1997). Nepotism and sexism in peer-review. *Nature*, 387, 341–343. DOI: 10.1038/387341a0. 15

White, H. D., Boell, S. K., Yu, H., Davis, M., Wilson, C. S., and Cole, F. T. H. (2009). Libcitations: A measure for comparative assessment of book publications in the humanities and social sciences. *Journal of the American Society for Information Science and Technology*, 60(6), 1083–1096. DOI: 10.1002/asi.21045. 38

Whitley, R. (2000). *The Intellectual and Social Organization of the Sciences* (2nd ed.). Oxford: Oxford University Press. 107

Wilkinson, D., Sud, P., and Thelwall, M. (2014). Substance without citation: Evaluating the online impact of grey literature. *Scientometrics*, 98(2), 797–806. DOI: 10.1007/s11192-013-1068-7. 49

Wilsdon, J. (2016). T*he Metric Tide: Independent Review of the Role of Metrics in Research Assessment and Management*. Oxford, UK: SAGE. 1

Wilson, E. B. (1927). Probable inference, the law of succession, and statistical inference. *Journal of the American Statistical Association*, 22(158), 209–212. DOI: 10.1080/01621459.1927.10502953. 114

Wouters, P. and Costas, R. (2012). Users, narcissism and control: Tracking the impact of scholarly publications in the 21st century. In: E. Archambault, Y. Gingras, V. Larivière (Eds) *Proceedings of the 17th International Conference on Science and Technology Indicators*, Montreal: ScienceMetrix and OST, 2, pp. 487–497. 20, 68

Yu, M. C., Wu, Y. C. J., Alhalabi, W., Kao, H. Y., and Wu, W. H. (2016). ResearchGate: An effective altmetric indicator for active researchers? *Computers in Human Behavior*, 55, 1001–1006. DOI: 10.1016/j.chb.2015.11.007. 28

Zahedi, Z., Fenner, M., and Costas, R. (2014a). How consistent are altmetrics providers? Study of 1000 PLOS ONE publications using the PLOS ALM, Mendeley and Altmetric. com APIs. In altmetrics 14. *Workshop at the Web Science Conference*, Bloomington, U.S. 34, 44

Zahedi, Z., Haustein, S., and Bowman, T. (2014b). Exploring data quality and retrieval strategies for Mendeley reader counts. Sigmet Metrics 2014 workshop, 5 November 2014. http://www.slideshare.net/StefanieHaustein/sigmetworkshop-asist2014. 83

Zimmermann, C. (2013). Academic rankings with RePEc. *Econometrics*, 1(3), 249–280. DOI: 10.3390/econometrics1030249. 20, 26

Zoller, D., Doerfel, S., Jäschke, R., Stumme, G., and Hotho, A. (2016). Posted, visited, exported: Altmetrics in the social tagging system BibSonomy. *Journal of Informetrics*, 10(3), 732–749. DOI: 10.1016/j.joi.2016.03.005. 45

Zuccala, A. and Guns, R. (2013). Comparing book citations in humanities journals to library holdings: Scholarly use versus perceived cultural benefit. In *14th International Conference of the International Society for Scientometrics and Informetrics* (pp. 353–360). 40

Zuccala, A., Guns, R., Cornacchia, R., and Bod, R. (2015a). Can we rank scholarly book publishers? A bibliometric experiment with the field of history. *Journal of the Association for Information Science and Technology*, 66(7), 1333–1347. DOI: 10.1002/asi.23267. 50

Zuccala, A. A., Verleysen, F. T., Cornacchia, R., and Engels, T. C. (2015b). Altmetrics for the humanities: Comparing Goodreads reader ratings with citations to history books. *Aslib Journal of Information Management*, 67(3), 320–336. DOI: 10.1108/AJIM-11-2014-0152. 38

Author Biography

Mike Thelwall is Professor of Information Science and leader of the Statistical Cybermetrics Research Group at the University of Wolverhampton, which he joined in 1989. He is also Docent at the Department of Information Studies at Åbo Akademi University, and a research associate at the Oxford Internet Institute. His Ph.D. was in Pure Mathematics from the University of Lancaster but he is now a social scientist focusing on quantitative methods. Mike has developed a wide range of methods for gathering and analysing web indicator data, most of which are available in the free software Webometric Analyst. His 550 publications include 280 refereed journal articles, 23 book chapters and two books, including *Introduction to Webometrics*. He is an associate editor of the *Journal of the Association for Information Science and Technology* and sits on three other editorial boards. He led the Wolverhampton contribution to the EU-funded projects Acumen, CyberEmotions RESCAR, CREEN, NetReAct, Rindicate and Wiser, and has been funded for research by JISC and non-profit organisations in the UK and Italy. He has also conducted evaluation contracts for the EC (several times), the UNDP (several times), the UNFAO and a UN university and was a member of the UK's independent review of the role of metrics in research assessment.

http://www.scit.wlv.ac.uk/~cm1993/mycv.html

Printed in the United States
by Baker & Taylor Publisher Services